EMPOWERED

TEEN SPIRIT

Edited By Jenni Harrison

First published in Great Britain in 2022 by:

Young Writers
Remus House
Coltsfoot Drive
Peterborough
PE2 9BF
Telephone: 01733 890066
Website: www.youngwriters.co.uk

All Rights Reserved
Book Design by Ashley Janson
© Copyright Contributors 2021
Softback ISBN 978-1-80015-764-4

Printed and bound in the UK by BookPrintingUK
Website: www.bookprintinguk.com
YB0492W

⭐ FOREWORD ⭐

Since 1991, here at Young Writers we have celebrated the awesome power of creative writing, especially in young adults where it can serve as a vital method of expressing their emotions and views about the world around them. In every poem we see the effort and thought that each student published in this book has put into their work and by creating this anthology we hope to encourage them further with the ultimate goal of sparking a life-long love of writing.

Our latest competition for secondary school students, Empowered, challenged young writers to consider what was important to them. We wanted to give them a voice, the chance to express themselves freely and honestly, something which is so important for these young adults to feel confident and listened to. They could give an opinion, share a memory, consider a dilemma, impart advice or simply write about something they love. There were no restrictions on style or subject so you will find an anthology brimming with a variety of poetic styles and topics. We hope you find it as absorbing as we have.

We encourage young writers to express themselves and address subjects that matter to them, which sometimes means writing about sensitive or contentious topics. If you have been affected by any issues raised in this book, details on where to find help can be found at www.youngwriters.co.uk/info/other/contact-lines

✷ CONTENTS ✷

Archway, Middlesbrough

George Cunningham (12)	1

Caludon Castle School, Wyken

Josh Adams (16)	2
Amber James (11)	5
Art Woodley (11)	6
Ollie Barratt (12)	7
Alfie McQueen (11)	8
Praise Akerele (12)	9
Ellenor Bench (12)	10
Jeevan Gill (11)	11
Alexa Kingham (12)	12
Maceo Mcleod (11)	13
Abishaya Ravindran	14
Mia Vyas (11)	15
Ryan Amarteifio	16
Ovya Ravindran	17
Dylan Keningale	18

Deyes High School, Maghull

Benjamin Bugg (12)	19
Olivia Jones (15) & Lucy	20
Chloe Watson (11)	22
Erin Potter (12)	23
Faye Crowther (12)	24
Zane Fallows (11)	26
Hallie Ward (11)	27
Megan Lightfoot (12)	28
Isabella Tuddenham (12)	30
Keira Akahoho (12)	31
Lillie Duke (11)	32
Amber Charnock (13)	33

Christina Orfanidi (15)	34
Holly Hughes (11)	35
Thomas Steele (11)	36
Lilly Daulbey (11)	37
Will Cliffe	38
Georgia Boyd (12)	39
Neve Charman (13)	40
Evan Wilson (11)	41
Lauren Cowell (12)	42
Erin Johnson (11)	43
Millie Roberts (13)	44
Freya Lovett (12)	45
Ruby Facer (13)	46
Joseph Dagnall (11)	47
Daisy Harding (12)	48
Owen Lloyd (12)	49
Zach Lloyd (11)	50
Adam Burns (11)	51
Lucy Graham (12)	52
Heidi Prendergast (11)	53
Holly Lightfoot (12)	54
Ellis Lindsay (12)	55
Megan Dykes (11)	56
Holly Ferris (11)	57
Chloe Allen (12)	58
Nathan Wagner (12)	59
Jayden Wheatcroft (12)	60
Rose Blakemore (12)	61
Frankie Crellin (12)	62
Max Wilson (12)	63
Thomas Trotter (11)	64
James Dagnall (11)	65
Faye Holliday (12)	66
Ethan Mitchell (12)	67
Millicent Carr-Richards (12)	68

Poppy Sutcliffe (11)	69
Ross Forsyth (13)	70
Sadie Kilmurry (11)	71
Evie O'Toole (11)	72
Poppy Byrnes (13)	73
Toni Branigan (11)	74
Ryan McLoughlin (11)	75
Adam Holme (11)	76
Liam Williams (12)	77
Laila Dris (12)	78
Emily Beach (12)	79
Summer McLeary (11)	80
Ruby Dolan (11)	81
Samuel Damota (12)	82
Frankie Scott (11)	83
Grace Warrilow (12)	84
Ruby Reeve (11)	85
Esme Pickles (11)	86
Zach Hogan (11)	87
Benjamin James Cowen (11)	88
Maxwell Hogan (11)	89
Thomas Aldridge (12)	90
Callum Murray (12)	91
Erin Chanman (11)	92
Finlay O'Nions (12)	93
Alanna White (12)	94
Zachary Lloyd (11)	95
Maizie Johnson (11)	96
Isabella Yanez (11)	97
Kieran Burness (12)	98
Jamie Mccloy (11)	99
Lexi Taylor (12)	100
Albert Stewart (11)	101
Mathew Hodgkiss (11)	102
Jack Clayton (12)	103
Natasha Dix (12)	104
Penny Mulholland (11)	105
Stephen Oyelowe	106
Alex Ainscough (11)	107
Harry Jones (12)	108
Owen Hamilton (11)	109
Ethan Kendrick (12)	110
Haydn Norris (11)	111
Owain Madoc-Jones (11)	112
Harrison McGuiness (11)	113
Charlie Doyle (12)	114
Joseph Willis (12)	115
George Cox (12)	116
Ava Boswell (11)	117
Faith Goodwin (11)	118
Zach Wooding (11)	119

Horizon Community College, Barnsley

Radomir Stamatov (15)	120
Emma Rutter (12)	123
Elena Iordan (13)	124
Darcie Stell (15)	126
Charlie Senior	128
Adam Oliver	130
Isaac-Jae Jackson	132
Kate Ledger (14)	134
Justin Howlett	136
Nathaniel Wathey (14)	137
Rebekah Carrington (14)	138
Faith Lumb (15)	139
Kirstie Bennett (14)	140
Holly Casken (14)	142
Harry Tordoff (14)	143
Beau Burrows (11)	144
Oliver Morgan (11)	146
Lilly Sephton (13)	147
Lily Hobbs	148
Izzy Gardham (13)	149
Elliot D E Clarke (13)	150
Bryony Jennings	151
Jessica Gosling (11)	152
Isabella Wilby (12)	153
Jasmine Burton (13)	154
Carla Macoviciuc	155
Senuli Perera (12)	156
Molly Holmes	157
Ashton Wilkinson (15)	158
Aaron Shah	159
Megan Lowes	160
Lily Graham (15)	161

Our Lady & St Bede Catholic Academy, Stockton-On-Tees

Emaan Anwar (11)	162
Codrin Catana (11)	164
Milo Knowles (13)	166
Hayley Paskin-Bell (14)	168
Emily Saint (14)	170
Raine Longstaff (14)	172
John Nicholson	173
Caroline Cummings (14)	174
Ashton Edwards (15)	175
Poppy Kelly (11)	176
Ellie Blackburn (15)	177
Muhammad Ayaan Waseem (11)	178
Jessica Chesser (15)	179
Calin Ionita (11)	180
Oscar Allan (11)	181
Evie Dixon (14)	182
Annabelle McGlade (11)	183
Noah Dixon (11)	184
Alice O'Connor (12)	185
Harry Woodcock (11)	186

St Cenydd Community School, Trecenydd

Leonna Roberts (13)	187
Lily Owen (13)	188
Robyn Hall (13)	190
James Clark (13)	191
Olivia Coghlan (14)	192
Caitlyn Ford (13)	193
Ash Evans (14)	194
Joshua Fouweather (13)	195

St George's CE School, Gravesend

Rhys Tadhunter (12), Jay & Charlie	196
Scarlett Trott (11)	197
James Allison (11)	198
Tyler Parker (15)	199

Mercedes Asamoah-Brown (13)	200
Sienna Dalton (13)	201
Nathan Bains (12)	202
Sahil Somani (13)	203
Kaila Mutenga (12)	204

Woodfarm High School, Thornliebank

Emma Somerville (12)	205
Olivia Leask (12)	206
Olivia Bowie (12)	207
Rachael Cassels (12)	208
Rachel Somerville (12)	209
Lauren Glennie (12)	210
Ella Fontaniere (12)	211
Angus Robert Paxton (12)	212
Lily Monaghan (12)	213
Crystal O'Hara (12)	214
Hayah Ahmed (12)	215
Sophie Smith (12)	216
Murray Griffen (12)	217
Conner Cai (12)	218
Amy Motherwell (11)	219
Eva Miller (12)	220
Euan Reid (12)	221
Alexander Ferns (12)	222
Jack Dickov (11)	223
Harry Paterson (12)	224

THE POEMS

One Day A Week

If only school was for one day a week,
the rest of the time I could have longer to sleep.
I'd get up at dinner time and go downstairs,
try and make me do school work, if you dare.
I'd make some dinner, a nice beef stew,
Then I'd flick on the Xbox and play FIFA 22.
After that, I'll play football outside,
but soon it's time for school work, I nearly cried.

George Cunningham (12)
Archway, Middlesbrough

Blossom

I remember you were adrift,
Entrapped within the cocoon that deceived you,
Bound by a world tied through injustice,
Injustice that turned into a deep depression,
The sentiment of weakness was all around,
Like a soldier, you needed salvation;
The interrogative light of reality, are you ready?

Distraught as one was to witness the terror engulfing your world,
Like trees imprisoning light for shade, it could be so easy to avoid,
The attributes seen within people that fend for their, and their similar, rights' takes you off-guard,
I can see you contemplating the famous message:
"Everybody for themselves."
As one of natural human ignorance,
Do you feel comfort?
Confidence?
Security?
Peace? Within the confines of your own livelihood.
Speak! I am in no need to make haste,
As my life has been spent not taking my time to waste
on issues that affect the world that brought me here,
And gave you the experiences to reflect on and cheer.

As Luther King described it,
"Riot is the language of the unheard."
You may arise in fear to allow the thoughts of those with stories to share, to inflict on your judgement.
The judgement that so refuses to be challenged, yet you call yourself humble,
To put yourself in the position of a citizen and victim of the war in Afghanistan,
To open your imaginative sphere to being segregated by the pigmentation of one's skin,
Or driven away from public facilities because of your identification.
I give you empathy,
As bright and peaceful as a setting sun,
As the likes of King, Yousafzai, Thunberg and Nkoli spread their influence,
Who were as once where you stand blinded now, considered weak among the grandeur of our Earth,
It takes little effort, even in no action beyond it, to tune in.

I have a dream...

I remember you were adrift,
Entrapped within the cocoon that deceived you,
Bound by a world tied through injustice,
Injustice that turned into a deep depression,
The sentiment of weakness was all around,
Like a soldier, you needed salvation;

The light shone through my dark cocoon,
Vibrant, beauteous wings emerge,
As a butterfly, my internal struggle is over.
As a butterfly, I am ready;
To blossom.

Josh Adams (16)
Caludon Castle School, Wyken

Empowered

You gave me strength
You gave me fitness at all lengths
You helped me when I tried a double
And told me off when I was in trouble.

You gave me skills on the bar
You gave me confidence that's led me far
You've helped me train, sometimes in vain
When we've been through routines again and again.

You gave me hope
You've helped me cope
When things were tough, you've supported me
Where I'd get to, we didn't foresee.

You gave me the gym
Where I've worked to the brim
You gave me advice
And you've been really nice.

You gave me spring to use on the vault
To help me bring on my somersault
We've put in the hours, to increase my power
You really have helped me to feel empowered.

Amber James (11)
Caludon Castle School, Wyken

What's It Like To Be Me?

My family think I'm special because
I am kind and care about people.
My mum says I am smart
And I have the most amazing brain.
My brain is different because I have autism,
This means that I am sensitive and very caring,
Sometimes I stand up for people and support them.
I love to learn,
Maths, Art, History and Geography.
My mind is like a sponge with all the knowledge.
I like order and sorting things out,
This helps me to sort my mind out.
My passions are running, gaming
And I love reading.
Knowledge is power.
I am patient
And my nan says I'm wise
And I speak my mind.
I am very honest with everyone.
I feel happy with myself
And I love being different.
My autism empowers me.

Art Woodley (11)
Caludon Castle School, Wyken

Forest Fire

Deep in the woods there was a fire
That burned with an evil desire
A desire to feed on the pain
A flame that would never retire
A pyre with eternal domain

And it said
"Why do you keep on feeding me?
You made this happen
why can't you see
There are golden treasures underneath
The air makes it so hard to breathe
you'll see"

Deep in the woods, the fire grew higher
The sticks would burn like a pyre
And only the dust and ashes remained
They whistled and snapped like a choir
While we sit at home, entertained

Ollie Barratt (12)
Caludon Castle School, Wyken

Brother

When you got sick, you lost your way
We stood by you every day.
We came to see you every day, in your bed where you lay
I held your hand, watched you smile
I could see you growing.

You came home and had a new friend
It was hard at first but we got there in the end
With our family support, you grew.

Over time, with our support and encouragement, your confidence grew
You had time to talk and play
You even got a job, woohoo
I am glad you have the confidence to fly
You are my brother again.

Alfie McQueen (11)
Caludon Castle School, Wyken

Being Black Is Part Of Me

I'm proud to be black,
It's part of me.
Being black is who I am,
Because it's how God made me.

It's important to me,
To stand out from the crowd.
I was made this way,
And for that, I can be proud.

In my life, I might face
Challenges that are hard to brace,
Because of fake rules put in place,
Imposed by society on people of my race.

But, no matter what I face,
It's always just a phase,
For I live by grace,
And I am my race.

Praise Akerele (12)
Caludon Castle School, Wyken

No

I'm normally a people-pleaser,
always saying yes.
Can you do this? Can you do that?
Can you go there? Return that here?
Can I borrow this? Can I use that?
Yes, yes, yes.
Today I'm saying, no!
I've had enough of pleasing people,
they take me for granted.
So I'm saying, do it yourself,
I don't want to do that.
Instead, I'm going to do what I want to do.
And that doesn't involve you.

Ellenor Bench (12)
Caludon Castle School, Wyken

All About Me

Hi, my name is Jeevan,
Yes, I know it rhymes with Steven,
I love playing paintball,
But I am just not tall enough for basketball,
I am 11 years old,
But my brain is the size of a seven-year-old's,
I attend Caludon Castle School,
Work is a lot of hassle,
I play for Binley Woods football team on the weekend,
We won 6-2,
Not surprisingly, our football kit is blue,
I hope you enjoyed this, this was all about me.

Jeevan Gill (11)
Caludon Castle School, Wyken

Strike Of Rebellion

Loss, of course, is imminent
Pain dimming to insanity
Clouding from the deceit of despotism
Decisions made without right

Words of walls prophesying death
Silent drums beating violently
Rumbling skies approach, with sly
Hounds of the depth howling with warning intent

Chains rattle as wrists slash
Voices dying but never faulting
Backs sore from valiant defiance
Grief shadowing 'til dawn.

Alexa Kingham (12)
Caludon Castle School, Wyken

Time

Time is a fickle thing,
our past decisions cannot be altered,
time affects all of us,
it is not something we can tamper with,
all of the past is set in stone,
seconds, hours, months, years,
all decide who we were
and what we will become,
as every moment is crucial
in the moulding of our lives.

Maceo Mcleod (11)
Caludon Castle School, Wyken

You

You're terrified to speak
You think you're weak
You have the freedom of the wind
You have the freedom of a bird
Your mind can go as far as the galaxies
Your heart is as pretty as the cosmos
Follow the path your heart takes you on
And the only person who says you can't is you.

Abishaya Ravindran
Caludon Castle School, Wyken

A Big Change

I miss primary school,
Being the oldest was quite cool,
I miss the teachers and Year 5s,
I don't know if I'll survive.

Secondary school is much bigger than my primary,
The stairs, the kids, there's so many,
I like it so far,
The teachers are treating us like a star.

Mia Vyas (11)
Caludon Castle School, Wyken

Basketball Youngster's Dream

Hours on hours
Playing in the park
Or back at home training
Until it turns dark

Dribbling
All for rewards
Screams of calls
They rebound off the backboard

Honouring our skills
Keeping it clean
These are all
A basketball youngster's dream.

Ryan Amarteifio
Caludon Castle School, Wyken

My Poem

Are they jealous?
Or is it true feelings?
Are they aware?
Or do they not care?

Are they in pain?
Are they under the rain?
Are they happy?
Are they chappy?

You are perfect,
And no one can change that.
You are not wrecked,
Just remember that!

Ovya Ravindran
Caludon Castle School, Wyken

Football

Football is my dream
Tottenham is my team
I train with my dad
He is football mad
I play on Sunday
And I train on a Monday.

Dylan Keningale
Caludon Castle School, Wyken

Just Be You

People are quite similar to stone,
They can be sculpted and moulded, smooth and sharp.
They can be changed, be remade, be destroyed,
But each sculpture is different, from the outside down to the core.

They can be carved from ice, from rock, from whatever they want.
Because no one is the same, even if only by a scratch,
Each person is different and better than the last.
No one should or can be the same,
Even if you try, you'll never get it just right all the way.

They are carved and chiselled, by school, family, blood and pain,
Trust me when I tell you that no one is the same.
No two people are alike, from what they've done to what they do,
Nobody else is just like you.

Like onions, like apples and sculptures too,
Their skin, their core, their small oddities and what they do,
No one is the same as anyone else,
So don't begin to try, give up and just be you.

Benjamin Bugg (12)
Deyes High School, Maghull

When You're Sixteen

When you're sixteen and when you're a girl,
you have the whole of society telling you
what you should and what you shouldn't do with your body.
They say, "Change your dress; it's too long, too short, too dull, too shiny."
These unrealistic standards have only increased dramatically
within today's male-dominated and social-media-obsessed society.
But this must change - we must make a statement.
That night, when you were at the party and the other girls kept staring...
The ones who said, "That colour isn't for you,"
"Your figure is off in that,"
"What a pretty dress! Not on you, maybe, but on me - yes."
Why listen?
Why take others' opinions on your appearance?
Why block out all of the compliments you received and focus on one negative comment?
Who cares if you don't have the hairstyle every girl desires?
Who cares if you don't keep up with the latest fashion trends?
Who cares if you are your true, authentic self?

Being your true self is what really matters.
It's your story.
You direct it
and others will follow.

Olivia Jones (15) & Lucy
Deyes High School, Maghull

All About Me

This poem will contain facts about me,
to start, the most important thing (to me) is family.
Even though family is my priority,
I still have lots of enjoyable hobbies.
The first one being sports,
my favourite sport being football.
Football makes me relaxed and at ease
whilst getting to play for my teams.
One big dream of mine
is to become a footballer and shine.
I also have two fluffy dogs
who love to play and cause chaos.
They both really love the park,
it looks like they could run for yards.

I also have friends to treasure
who help relieve all kinds of pressure.
They are the best people I've ever met,
almost as good as my fluffy pets.
I'm really at a high now,
if you're not, I don't know how.
Remember how much you are loved,
if you think you can't succeed, you always could.

Chloe Watson (11)
Deyes High School, Maghull

My Mates

You should love your friends and I'll tell you why
If you treat them well, they'll never lie
They help me with work when I'm stuck
And support me through times that are tough

They cheer me up when I am low
And my kindness is what I need to show
If I never walked through the school gate
I would have never been proud to call you my mate

They are also so helpful, so caring and kind
And that is all that goes on in my mind
We walk to school together every day
So, thank you, is all I want to say

Weekends are made to hit the shops
And on the train, we count the stops
All we do is spend, bags galore
We've walked so far, our feet are sore

They always make me laugh, even when I feel down
They make me smile and take away my frown
So, this is why you need to have friends
Because that kindness will never end.

Erin Potter (12)
Deyes High School, Maghull

You

You don't need to be gorgeous,
You don't need to be pretty,
You don't need to be smart,
You don't need to be witty.
There is no one like you,
You're special, you're rare,
You're the only you,
From your feet to your hair.
If you're a boy or girl,
Or anything in-between,
Be you! Don't change,
You're fabulous! I've seen
Others who are rude,
Others who are mean,
Others who are selfish,
So I'm not very keen.
We all get moody,
We all whine,
But as long as you're not horrible,
You'll sparkle, you'll shine.
What I'm trying to say is,
Be kind, be gentle,
Don't be spiteful,
Don't go mental.

Stay the way you are,
You're perfect, you see,
Don't change to be like him,
Her, or me!

Faye Crowther (12)
Deyes High School, Maghull

Homeless People

Social responsibility, where is it?
You have to look after the homeless,
everyone is different,
you shouldn't be so quick to judge them.
You don't know what it's like to be homeless until you have walked in their shoes.

Social responsibility, where is it?
Why is it that rich people think that homeless people are bad?
We are all human.
Rich people also look down at homeless people and say,
"Why would I give you my money?
You are just going to buy drugs and alcohol."
But how would they know that?
Every homeless person has a story to tell.

Social responsibility, where is it?
Rich people reject homeless people,
but they are rejecting humanity.
If I were in that situation,
I would rather be poor and happy than rich and very dull.

Zane Fallows (11)
Deyes High School, Maghull

Take The Mask Away

When I feel down and there is no one around
I always wonder if I should be proud
The effort and time it takes to wrap myself in a face
That no one else ever needed to trace.
I always try to smile away the tears that fall
And I try to show no sign of weakness at all.
All the hating and debating just to know
That I've been hiding behind a mask
And that should be the end of it all.
The mask then falls and I then thought my life can go to a new resort.
Through all those thoughts and being caught along the way
At least now I know there is nothing with my display each night
I always thought, *will I ever be the girl I was taught?*
But now the mask is gone, I'm now self-loving
And so now I share the face I never thought I'd learn to misplace!

Hallie Ward (11)
Deyes High School, Maghull

What Have We Done To Earth?

The Earth is slipping
through our fingers,
like the globe has been knocked off balance
and we are tipping it further.

The colours of the world
that used to be
are now buried
beneath our towering cities.

The air outside is suffocating,
a great grey smoke fills the streets,
people take and steal and hurt and kill
over the remaining animals and trees.

The Amazon seemed everlasting,
vast and green like it was always growing,
but we were greedy
and now it is gone.

The ice caps have melted,
the oceans are dry,
but our world leaders
continue to lie.

Doomsday is coming
and we aren't prepared,
the planet is crumbling,
and I fear for our world
and everything within it.

Megan Lightfoot (12)
Deyes High School, Maghull

In The Mirror She Sees

When she looks in the mirror, all she can see,
a basic girl but not the one she wants to be.
She doubts, she shouts
she cries, she sighs
look at her figure as I tell her to reconsider
what she sees in the mirror

I tell her
we grow like a tree,
we change, we range
feel confident in who you are.
Don't care for what others think and just remember
your human self
is a work of art

not everybody's the same,
otherwise that would just be plain.
Wishing to be someone else
isn't good for your health.

So remember to love yourself!

Then she looked in the mirror, all she could see
was a bold, beautiful girl
that she had always wanted to be!

Isabella Tuddenham (12)
Deyes High School, Maghull

Believe

When you're feeling blue,
And a wave of doubt washes over you,
Just remember this,
And you'll never feel amiss.

Take a button for example,
They're all different shapes and sizes,
Different colours and appearances,
Much like humans.

On the outside, we're all different,
Different sizes and shapes,
Different colours and appearances,
But we're all the same on the inside.

So just believe in yourself,
Be proud to stand out,
Everyone is equal,
So feel empowered and remember

When you're feeling blue,
And a wave of doubt washes over you,
Just remember this,
And you'll never feel amiss,
Believe.

Keira Akahoho (12)
Deyes High School, Maghull

Our World

Shy or timid, that's not me!
The sky is my limit,
Never-ending.
Lending a hand is what my family do.
This is my identity, it always will be.
It's not fair that people are treated differently,
Repeated unfairness,
Girl or boy,
Careless words that are thrown around hurt.
Discrimination...
You're too young,
You're too annoying,
You're too old,
You're too stupid,
Girl or boy,
Careless words that are thrown around hurt.
Everyone is different, like a tree.
No bark is the same as another.
No branch is the same as another.
No leaf is the same as another.
Why would we change for someone else?
There is only one me.

Lillie Duke (11)
Deyes High School, Maghull

The Earth

The Earth is dying because of us,
Climate change, littering and deforestation,
Forests are burning and glaciers are melting,
Animals are losing their habitats
Due to loss of trees and build-up of rubbish.

The environment is changing and it's all our fault,
Overconsumption of products, poaching and pollution,
Waste in the ocean and on the beach,
Animals are killed for money
And global warming is becoming dangerous.

Our planet is damaged and we need to save it,
Try walking instead of driving
And put your litter in a bin,
Use less plastic and reuse and recycle,
If we all work together, we can revive the Earth,
Back to all its former glory.

Amber Charnock (13)
Deyes High School, Maghull

Overcoming The Darkness

My mind has a pest,
It's like a chaotic mess.
It fills me with doubt,
I just want to shout.
Screaming, crying
Help me... I think I'm dying -
I'm drowning in sorrow...
Will I even be here tomorrow?
The battlefield of my mind is in decline.
They ask me how I am... *Fine!*
I start to plummet into a darkness so great,
Until one lesson I looked at my mate.
I had my teachers, friends and family for support,
And that's when I came up with a brilliant thought.
I want to appreciate all that I own,
My life is worth living - I'm no longer alone.
I want to show people that they can heal,
Even if right now that may seem surreal.

Christina Orfanidi (15)
Deyes High School, Maghull

A Letter To Our World

Dear our world,
Listen up, I am not happy, we are ripping you to pieces bit by bit.
We are tearing you apart, to pieces, and that's not it.
The plants are rotting and what was once fresh green grass is dying.
The warm blue seas in the ocean are rising.
We are taking the animals from their homes
Just for one amusement; don't tell me that's not wrong.
So everyone in the world, listen up.
Enough is enough.
It is time to change the world for the best
So that children in 1,000 years can have a single breath.
Recycle and do not litter
Or our lives will all turn bitter.
Now let's change our world for a greater future.

Holly Hughes (11)
Deyes High School, Maghull

The Doodle Poem

As a boy who likes to doodle,
I find it interesting
To grab some paper
And then a pen,
Then doodle to my heart's delight.

A frog then a man,
Oh, what in the heavens will come next?
Dragons and people and animals
All at the top of the list to draw.

Stickmen to cars to dogs
Looks like they come next
Followed by plants and cats
Then rats and bats.

Oh, what comes next?
But don't dread
Just as it is only a giant pie.

But I must confess
That at the bottom of the list
Has to be spiders.

And that's the poem
Of the doodling boy.

Thomas Steele (11)
Deyes High School, Maghull

To The People Who Inspires Me

If you were in front of me these are the things I would want to say.
I am so happy you inspire me every day,
You always help me when I'm stuck or need help
And for that, I want to say thank you.

When I feel sad you always inspire me and have time to talk to me.
When our pets die you help me and always make me feel better.
You gave me a home and you try your best for me every day
And for that, I want to thank you.

You gave me brothers and a sister.
When I feel lonely you always make me happy.
You make every day better and you make me smile
And for that, I want to say thank you.

Lilly Daulbey (11)
Deyes High School, Maghull

Mo Salah Poem

Mo Salah is the best,
Forget about Messi and Ronaldo, they need to take a rest.

He runs down the wing
While the Anfield crowds sing.
He will run past Kyle Walker
And stick the ball in the top corner.

He wears the Liverpool shirt with pride,
And takes everything in his stride.
All the children getting kits that have his name,
It just never gets lame.

I can't get around how he's so good,
He just leaves us speechless and the defenders in the mud.

There's no one better in his position,
Don't stop him, he's on a mission.

Will Cliffe
Deyes High School, Maghull

We Are Human

We are human.
People who are sick,
Feel worthless, helpless, stuck,
They can't escape.

They go out
And people stare.
They are embarrassed
And are not comfortable in public,
They feel like they are an animal.

I don't matter,
I am a breathing mannequin,
I am vulnerable,
I am a mouse in a box,
This is it for the rest of my life.

It's okay,
You are normal,
You do matter,
You aren't vulnerable,
You are perfect.

Just because they have a disability
Doesn't mean they are not human.

Georgia Boyd (12)
Deyes High School, Maghull

Dementia's Story

Dementia affects many lives,
Including mine and my family's.
My grandad is going through dementia
And it's like his memory is floating away
Like the leaves of a dandelion.
Every time I see him I think,
What if he doesn't remember me?
I have a little cousin who is three,
And by the age of six, my grandad may not remember him.
Dementia is a slow and painful process.
I mean, watching your loved one
Not even remembering you exist is miserable and sorrowful.
I want to spread awareness
Because it may help thousands just like my grandad.

Neve Charman (13)
Deyes High School, Maghull

My Lovely Mummy

Some people can be dark inside
but with my mum, it's a whole new ride.
From a life of gifts and lots of trips
but that doesn't matter,
as long as my mum is with me.
When I see my mum, I greet her with a hug,
then I feel as soft as a bug.
She inspires me to do well,
I always feel a wave of hope,
not feeling like I'm tied in a rope.
But all I need to know is that my mum is still with me,
we are closer to the end
but I can say, mums throw you round the bend
or drive you nuts.
But all that matters is, our mums are still with us.

Evan Wilson (11)
Deyes High School, Maghull

Climate Change

If climate change doesn't change, what will happen?
Animals will suffer and die,
Icebergs will melt, leaving polar bears to cry.

If climate change doesn't change, what will happen?
The ozone layer will become thin,
If we don't change now, we will never win.

If climate change doesn't change, what will happen?
The Earth is heating up fast,
Let's hope it's all in the past.

If climate change doesn't change, what will happen?
We can all do small things to help,
To save this Earth before it's too late.

Lauren Cowell (12)
Deyes High School, Maghull

60 Seconds With A Racist Brain

If I had 60 seconds with a racist brain
I would make him feel ashamed
I would tell him we're all the same
And maybe he would reflect on what I said, and change

I would tell him everyone deserves peace
And to be racist is the least
I would tell him to become the least racist person there is
And that people's problems are none of his biz'

I would tell him to keep all his thoughts in his head
And hope that they would become dead
And in the last few seconds that we're in
I'd tell him to put racism in the bin.

Erin Johnson (11)
Deyes High School, Maghull

You Are

Happiness, an amazing emotion
One felt by a person unbroken
But many people are unable to feel this way
And remain grim throughout their days.

But remember, if you are one of these people
You are brave, powerful and free like an eagle
Do not allow the chains to bind you
Speak out, let it show, for only then will someone find you.

Never forget that you are loved
You are special, you are beautiful, soar high
And free in the sky, up above
And do not let your hope be devoured,
For you are not weak, you are empowered.

Millie Roberts (13)
Deyes High School, Maghull

You Are Who You Are

You are who you are.
We are all different.
Yet in some ways we are the same.
We all breathe the same air,
We all need food and water.
We are all human but still we are different.
Whether it's the colour of your skin,
If you are a girl or a boy,
If you have brown eyes or blue,
You are never exactly the same as everybody else.

You are who you are,
Anyone can do what they aspire to do,
If they want to fly like a bird they can.
You are a star among other stars,
Start letting your real shimmer shine through.

Freya Lovett (12)
Deyes High School, Maghull

You Are Who You Are

Empowerment,
Everyone is unique just like a snowflake,
No one is the same, so don't be fake,
Every day you are awake,
Enjoy your life because you are who you are!

Everyone is unique just like a butterfly,
No one is the same, so please don't cry,
One day, we're all going to die,
So enjoy your life,
Because you are who you are!

Everyone is unique, so do what you do,
No one is the same, so just be you,
Sometimes in life, you will feel blue,
But enjoy your life,
Because you are who you are!

Ruby Facer (13)
Deyes High School, Maghull

Is Perfection Real?

One day I sat and pondered,
By that I mean truly wondered,
I started to think, I started to feel,
What if perfection was never real?
As for every high, and every score,
There was always at least a single flaw.
And for every award, every trophy on the shelf,
Is that really being yourself?
You might be messy, with a room all clean,
You might be shy, but carry a certain gleam.
So why doesn't anybody see?
You're the best you that you can be!
So in conclusion, I will say,
Everybody can be their own special way.

Joseph Dagnall (11)
Deyes High School, Maghull

Kindness Gives Confidence

Braveness is not easy to use and do,
Sometimes confidence is the clue.
People smiling can lighten up your day
And getting compliments can make you feel some type of way.
People like hanging out with friends
And people like to party alone
But at the end of the day, we all need a bit of confidence.
It makes you feel like you're on top of the world
When you think you look nice,
Especially when you get good advice.
So please just think,
You being kind could potentially
Change the sad thoughts in people's minds.

Daisy Harding (12)
Deyes High School, Maghull

Dear Future Me

Dear future me,
You're as happy as can be.
You have your ups and you have your downs,
But you shouldn't wear a frown.

Dear future me,
I hope you have wealth,
Are you able to drive
Or do you still have to thrive?

Dear future me,
Are you still full of glee?
Do you have your own home
And do you live alone?

Dear future me,
Do you have your awards on a shelf?
Did you do good at school
Or did you act like a fool?

Dear future me,
Be the best you can be.

Owen Lloyd (12)
Deyes High School, Maghull

Love Yourself

Although no two people are the same, we all want one thing,
to love and be loved.
Even though we all are, we may not love ourselves,
you may not believe me but difference is to be celebrated.

Who would want to love in a world where we are all the same?
Nothing to talk about, nothing to share.
Nobody would want to live in a world so lame,
if everyone was the same, would you think that would be fair?

I like that I am different,
and so should you.
I like that you are different,
and so should you.

Zach Lloyd (11)
Deyes High School, Maghull

Our Planet

We need to look after our planet and protect the bees,
the butterflies and other species.
By planting flowers, green grass and edible plants,
we all need to take a stance.
Climate change is having an effect on the world,
with all the seasons mixed into a whirl.
We all need to reduce, reuse or recycle as much as we can,
glass, paper, plastic and tin cans.
We need to stop polluting the air
and educate those around us to take more care.
We all must play our part,
so please, please, let's make a start.

Adam Burns (11)
Deyes High School, Maghull

If There Was An Ideal World

If I could take over the world
What would I do?
I would make everyone equal
No matter, race or ethnicity.

I would make global warming disappear
It would stop many animals from becoming extinct
I would stop world and civil wars
Preventing hatred amongst all.

I would give to those in need
Bringing a light into their lives
I would help refugees
Giving them a safe place to live.

What would I do
If I took over the world
I would make a change
A change for the better.

Lucy Graham (12)
Deyes High School, Maghull

Don't Change

Many people wish they were beautiful
Or want to change the way they look,
But don't change yourself.
Everyone is amazing just the way they are.
Even though you think people look better than you
That doesn't mean you should change yourself to look a bit like them.
People are like flowers,
Some want to be different and some want to be taller,
Some want to be shorter
But everyone is beautiful in their own way,
Just like flowers.
Its beauty within you not on the outside of you that counts.

Heidi Prendergast (11)
Deyes High School, Maghull

Speak Up For Your Rights

To those who don't have a voice,
You should speak up for your rights,
No matter who you are or what you want,
You should speak up for your rights.

Whether you are male or female,
Black or white,
Young or old, LGBTQ+ or not,
You should speak up for your rights.

Everyone is still fighting for their rights,
For what they do and don't want,
You should speak for yourself
And stand with others in the fight for rights,
You should speak up for your rights.

Holly Lightfoot (12)
Deyes High School, Maghull

Dear Future Me

Dear future me,
How is life now?
Have I travelled the sea?
How is Bruce doing... *Miaow!*

Is England a great country,
Is Freya still loud,
Do we still live with our family,
Does Freya still have a large crowd?

Dear future me,
Is Mia still cheeky,
Have I bought my own house with its own house key,
Does she still dress the dog up freaky?

Dear future me,
How did I do in school?
Did I do outstanding
Or did I fail like a fool?

Ellis Lindsay (12)
Deyes High School, Maghull

Until The End

This is a poem about my friends,
The ones that stuck until the end.
The ones that stayed for the good times and bad,
The ones that loved me when I was mad.

This is a poem about my friends,
The ones that stuck until the end.
The ones that I can rely on day and night,
The ones that make the darkness light.

This is a poem about my friends,
The ones that stuck until the end.
The ones that love me for who I can be,
The ones that love me because I'm me.

Megan Dykes (11)
Deyes High School, Maghull

Differences

D on't think you're different
I magine being like everyone else
F amous celebrities aren't excellent
F ootballers' penalties are never the same
E veryone is different
R unners run at different speeds
E ven the discoloured, misshapen apple seeds
N o one looks or thinks like you do
C ould only you be the best you?
E veryone is the same on the inside
S o accept yourself for who you are?

Holly Ferris (11)
Deyes High School, Maghull

Empowered

Feeling empowered is to look in the mirror
and like what you see,
whoever the person you are staring at
may be.

It comes from within and you beam
with pride,
you can feel this power
shining bright inside.

This power is contagious,
it spreads positive vibes
and it attracts people
from all kinds of tribes.

So let's empower each other
and all stand up,
and help up others
who have been unlucky to fall.

Chloe Allen (12)
Deyes High School, Maghull

Plastic Is The Problem

It may look simple, plastic,
but the effects are drastic.
Pollution in the world's oceans,
mixing together like toxic potions.
As another animal dies,
nobody listening to their cries.
On the seas it is imperial,
a poisonous material,
it takes no prisoners
like an evil visitor.
But what if we eased the world's pain?
And made a healthy food chain,
because fewer polymers in the world's oceans
would be better for you and me.

Nathan Wagner (12)
Deyes High School, Maghull

You've Been There For Me

All those times we've had a laugh,
Watching TV shows.
And I know you're good at maths,
But you can be a show-off.

You've always been there for me,
Even when I only scratched my knee,
And all those times you've helped me complete a video game,
Even if you thought some of them were lame.

So now after all the times you've helped me,
I'm going to help you,
You can beat it,
Cancer doesn't stand a chance.

Jayden Wheatcroft (12)
Deyes High School, Maghull

The Beginning Of The End

Change your actions before climate change strikes,
there will be no more 'nature hikes',
the world is ending, slowly but surely,
all the animals are going extinct,
look back to the past,
look how it's all linked.
Soon pollution will be the new sea,
and people will cut down every single tree,
our world is ending,
it needs a lot of mending.
Climate change,
animal extinction,
pollution,
it's the beginning of the end.

Rose Blakemore (12)
Deyes High School, Maghull

Respect

Learn to be respectful,
love the way you are,
don't let anyone tell you different,
shine like a star.

Learn to be respectful
for those around you,
everyone is different,
but we're all the same too.

Learn to be respectful,
everyone has rights,
don't take them away
or I will put up a fight.

Learn to be respectful
for everyone, even you,
it's very important
and now you know what to do.

Frankie Crellin (12)
Deyes High School, Maghull

Empowered

H ave a heart and do your part,
E ndangered animals living in fear,
L isten up then,
P lay your part,

T hey shouldn't be worn,
H owever, they should be playing,
E ach jumping around,
M ore must be done,

L earn about them for them
I nform your friends and family
V ets should be called if an animal is hurt
E mpower others to save animals too.

Max Wilson (12)
Deyes High School, Maghull

Football

Football.
How does it feel to play football?
How does it feel to win a game?
How does it feel to be part of a team?

Football.
The excitement. The thrill. The joy.
Being part of a team is being part of a family.
Winning a game has a feeling you never want to let go.

Football.
Goal! Scoring a goal is what every player wants in football.
The crowd cheering, chanting your name.
All this makes football the game it is.

Thomas Trotter (11)
Deyes High School, Maghull

Walkers Crisps

Walkers crisps,
They're crunchy, full of flavour,
They're the only food you'll ever need.

Walkers crisps,
So many flavours to savour,
They are like your very own lightsaber.

Walkers crisps,
Their quality and freshness
Makes you feel like your very own princess.

There's baked, normal and glorious too,
For over 100 years they've been a treat,
That you have to have at your midnight feast.

James Dagnall (11)
Deyes High School, Maghull

Who Am I?

Who am I?
What am I trying to be?
Definitely not myself,
My uniqueness needs to fly free.

Who am I?
I'm someone trying to believe,
I need to embrace myself,
I will achieve.

Who am I?
I'm a person who has come to see,
I'm perfect how I am,
All I needed to do was be me.

Who am I?
I have officially found the key,
I'm who I was born to be,
My uniqueness has flown free.

Faye Holliday (12)
Deyes High School, Maghull

I Wish I Was Our Charlie

I wish I was my Charlie.
Our Charlie is nearly six.
He gets away with everything.
Even smashing the window.
That's impossible for me.
I'm nearly thirteen.
Sometimes I can't stand our Charlie.
He always follows me around
wherever I go.
I feel like locking him in a pound.
I'm nearly thirteen,
Y'know our Charlie?
He's a big snitch.
He put us in the ditch.
He called my auntie a witch!

Ethan Mitchell (12)
Deyes High School, Maghull

Alone

It all happened quickly,
She was fine, then she lost it all.
Hoping the pain would blow over swiftly,
Freedom was blocked by a wall.

She lost her friends,
Her happiness as she watched the past fade.
She still smiled though,
No matter how she felt, unhappy or betrayed.

She felt lost and scared as people hurry past.
The only place she wanted to be was home.
She felt friendless and lonely.
She was all alone.

Millicent Carr-Richards (12)
Deyes High School, Maghull

Empowered

Empowered,
it's a great choice you make
to be the most empowered person you can be.
And it's all the choices you make
because you are the empowered one
and that is no mistake.
You can climb the highest mountain,
you can travel through the whole wide world
but you are still the empowered one.
We are all unique in our own way
but you are still the empowered one that controls your life
in a wholly unique way.

Poppy Sutcliffe (11)
Deyes High School, Maghull

If I Had A Magic Wand

If I had a magic wand, the first thing I would do
is find a cure for cancer
and stop climate change too.
If I had a magic wand, the next thing I would do
is stop the sun from exploding
and end racism too.
If I had a magic wand, the third thing I would do
is stop the moon from orbiting Earth
and keep it where it is.
If I had a magic wand, the last thing I would do
is to put a stop to Covid
and fix the world itself.

Ross Forsyth (13)
Deyes High School, Maghull

Equal Rights

Everybody has rights.
No matter your race or how you look
or if you're a girl or a boy,
everybody has rights.
You have the right to live, equal treatment,
the right to privacy,
the right to marry and have a family and freedom of thought.
Nobody can take that away from you,
it's almost your own prized possession.
No matter the differences, we all have the right.
If you ever feel that has been violated, speak up!

Sadie Kilmurry (11)
Deyes High School, Maghull

Equality

No matter how big or small,
we shouldn't judge bodies at all.

We are all bold and bright
and all need to shine our light.

No matter if black or white or in-between
that doesn't bother me.

You may have two mums or two dads.
You may have spots or scars.
That doesn't mean you don't play your part.

You may be different to everybody else
but that's what life's all about.

Evie O'Toole (11)
Deyes High School, Maghull

Girls' Footy

My opinion is that
Girls' footy is great
Also, it's fun and enjoyable
Playing with your teammates

Most people assume
Girls shouldn't play
But my opinion is different
Than most people's perspective

My idol is Steph Houghton
She plays for England
It's my dream to
One day be like her

Playing for England
Being like her.
I believe in equal
Rights.

Poppy Byrnes (13)
Deyes High School, Maghull

Dear Covid

Covid, how it damaged the world,
And it wasn't the best.
Family were always there,
People died,
People survived,
Family were always there,
From the cries and the sighs,
To the smiles I have shared,
Family were always there,
Covid is just like a bad friend,
The more you fight back the quicker it will go,
To the ones who had Covid,
Family were always there,
The point is... family overpowers Covid.

Toni Branigan (11)
Deyes High School, Maghull

The Picture

Ambitions begin,
Hopes for the future,
From once hated to an idol,
Although hope is indeed just a picture for the future,
An image of equal rights, with no hate,
A climate made just for me,
But although this will be nice,
I'm not the only artist with beer to drink,
With fear alive,
From cowards to heroes,
And love to hate,
But regardless...
The real picture is already painted for you...
Family.

Ryan McLoughlin (11)
Deyes High School, Maghull

Do The Best You Can Do

You need to be as firm as a tree,
That's what inspires me!
You have to accept others,
As if they're your brothers!
You're better than you were yesterday
And I hope that skill will stay!
Only stop when you're satisfied,
Then you know you've really tried.
It doesn't matter if people are better than you,
Hang on to that passion
And try to stay true.
Now that's what could inspire you.

Adam Holme (11)
Deyes High School, Maghull

Shell

When a turtle is threatened, they hide in their shell
But quite quickly this becomes a cell,
They hide and wait for a long time.

In this time they fear everything.
They forget that they are the king,
Their claws are long,
Their teeth are sharp,
They forget that they are powerful.

But the fact is, just remember
They will always come out of their shell,
And to their fear
They must say farewell.

Liam Williams (12)
Deyes High School, Maghull

You Matter

It's okay to be different,
It's okay to be unique,
No matter your shape,
No matter your size,
Whether it's the colour of your skin or the culture you believe in,
You still have rights and you deserve them!
You can love who you want,
And have the gender you want,
You shouldn't be judged by gender,
Or disabilities,
Oppression happens to a lot of people
And, no matter what,
You matter!

Laila Dris (12)
Deyes High School, Maghull

Save The Planet

Where will the world be
In 100 years?
If people don't start changing,
It'll be gone, just wait and see

People are destroying the rainforest,
Tearing down animals' homes,
Killing poor defenceless trees,
Destroying the ozone dome.

Everyone needs to step up and change,
Greta Thunberg has the right idea,
There's only one Earth, we need to save it,
Could I be any more clear?

Emily Beach (12)
Deyes High School, Maghull

Be Empowered

Nurses are like angels, doctors are like gods,
Policemen and firemen are like real-life superheroes!
Volunteers and charity workers give their free time to help people in need,
And the list goes on and on.
Life role models like Raheem Sterling and Marcus Rashford inspire people
To go and help their community,
They are not just footballers and idols,
They are lifesavers.
Anything can happen when you are empowered.

Summer McLeary (11)
Deyes High School, Maghull

Follow Your Hopes And Dreams

People need to follow their hopes and dreams
To achieve the person who you want to be
No matter who you are,
You were meant to be a star
Whoever says there's no point
Just remind them who you are
You are you with your hopes and dreams
No matter who, you are bound to have dreams
Just follow your heart and wish away
Follow your hopes and dreams and one day
They will come true
If you just be you!

Ruby Dolan (11)
Deyes High School, Maghull

I Dream Of Hope

I dream of a world with peace everywhere
A world where joy is always there
Hope never lost, showing me a good future
Where unity breaks division and a new culture is born
Equality and respect being part of all we do
Tolerance for being different, my view, skin or appearance
We are all one, our bodies, mind and spirit
It will get better, I hope it and I know
Perseverance is my friend,
The only way to go.

Samuel Damota (12)
Deyes High School, Maghull

Empowered

Liverpool is red, Everton is blue,
Football is a friendly sport created for you.
It has fans upon fans and players against players,
If you don't fit in that is alright
But if you do fit in join us and play.
It doesn't matter what gender you are,
You're always free to play,
Whether you're a boy or a girl,
Or if you have a disability,
It makes no difference,
Football is for everyone.

Frankie Scott (11)
Deyes High School, Maghull

Our Society

A generation full of damaged souls,
A person with a good heart is yet to be found.

Loyalty is rare and therefore trust is not given.
Forgiveness?
There is no such thing.

Boundaries of social etiquette are normal to transgress.
Love is a weakness and relationships are a mess.
Hatred roams amongst us all,
Hurting our dearest because of pride,
Regrets and apologies only once they have died.

Grace Warrilow (12)
Deyes High School, Maghull

Friends

Friendships come and friendships go,
But I know ours won't ever end.
You're fun, you're kind, you're sweet,
You're loyal,
But most of all, you make me laugh,
You make me smile, you make me happy,
Our friendship will never become too old,
When we met in Reception,
We had an instant connection,
And that will never ever stop, in forever,
This friendship, no one will ever sever.

Ruby Reeve (11)
Deyes High School, Maghull

If I Had A Magic Wand

If I had a magic wand,
I'd help the people who need it,
To give them love, a place to go,
When they don't think they deserve it.

All people need a hand, at one time or another,
It's just about telling the right people who will bother,
If you ever feel stranded,
Know that you are your best self,
And no one can say different.

We are all unique,
No matter what we seek.

Esme Pickles (11)
Deyes High School, Maghull

My Gaming Adventure

Waking up on a Sunday,
I know it will be a fun day.
As I get out of bed,
Just one thought goes through my head.
I skid downstairs,
It won't be long,
Until my computer sings its song.

My heart nearly skips a beat,
As I sit in my gaming seat,
Logging on to stream,
I'm nearly bursting at the seam.
Now on 'Cat Goes Fishing',
My adventure was just beginning.

Zach Hogan (11)
Deyes High School, Maghull

I'm The Prime Minister For A Day

I'm the prime minister for a day,
I'm a role model,
I'm powerful,

I'm the prime minister for a day,
I'm a role model,
I'm powerful,
I'm a ruler of a country,

I'm the prime minister for a day,
I'm a role model,
I'm powerful,
I'm a ruler of a country,
I'm a celebrity,

I'm the prime minister for a day.

Benjamin James Cowen (11)
Deyes High School, Maghull

We Are Earth's Predators

The ice caps are melting,
The polar bears' habitat is shrinking,
The air is being polluted,
The ocean is full of plastic,
We need to save the Earth.

We need to recycle,
We need to produce less greenhouse gases,
We need to stop putting plastic in the ocean,
We need to stop polluting our big beautiful planet,
We need to save the Earth.

We are Earth's predators.

Maxwell Hogan (11)
Deyes High School, Maghull

I Want To Be A Footballer

I want to be a footballer
And play in a gigantic stadium,
I want to play in the snow,
While me and my teammates put on a show.

I want to be a footballer
And to dribble like Mo Salah,
While the wind is a howling wolf,
I want to score a last-minute winner.

I want to be a footballer
And be rich,
But first I'll have to work hard in training
And on the pitch.

Thomas Aldridge (12)
Deyes High School, Maghull

Our Difference Together

We may all look so different
But only on the outside,
Yet people still just don't see it.
Gender or race,
It does not matter,
People are the same,
Just look different.
Suicides, unhappiness
Increasing rapidly,
All cos of two words...
'You're ugly'.
When will people realise
It doesn't matter what you look like
It just matters who you are.

Callum Murray (12)
Deyes High School, Maghull

That Little Bit Of Faith

You give me hope,
You give me strength.
Anxiety is a hard thing to go through
But with my friends and family by my side
I know I can do anything.

Have hope, have love and you can do anything
You give me courage and you love me.
Don't give up, you got this,
Through thick and thin I know you will win.

Be you, be kind,
And have that little bit of faith.

Erin Chanman (11)
Deyes High School, Maghull

Racism

The world is divided,
No one knows how to fix it,
No one can control others,
That's why I decided to write this poem.
People don't get a chance,
They fall into these stereotypes on who they are
And what they do.
Discrimination of race - racism
Only knowing what is expected of them,
Not being allowed to change who they are,
And getting abused for who they are.

Finlay O'Nions (12)
Deyes High School, Maghull

You're Glowing

If you feel down,
Go look in a mirror,
And you will see a beautiful smile.

If you feel down,
Think to yourself,
Is this really worth freaking out over?

If you feel down,
Tell someone and they can help you
Because you're their no. 1.

If you feel down,
Don't start bawling,
Just say to yourself, "You're glowing!"

Alanna White (12)
Deyes High School, Maghull

Environment

- **E** arth is in danger if we do not stop,
- **N** ature is suffering,
- **V** aquitas are dying,
- **I** cebergs are falling,
- **R** enewable energy is useful,
- **O** xygen is reducing,
- **N** atural resources diminishing,
- **M** other Nature is not happy,
- **E** co-systems crashing,
- **N** itrogen dioxide contaminating,
- **T** he sea is polluting.

Zachary Lloyd (11)
Deyes High School, Maghull

It's The Beauty That Comes Within

Image is not important,
You should love the way you are,
No matter your shape or size,
Or even a body filled with scars,
Never change yourself for others,
Because nobody is perfect,
So never let anyone
Treat you like an object,
No matter your gender or colour,
We all have our rights,
So don't let them take you down,
And together we will unite.

Maizie Johnson (11)
Deyes High School, Maghull

Thank You

Dear Mum and Dad,
Thank you for all,
You pacified me when I was bored.
Dear Mum and Dad,
Thank you again,
You bought me a dog
And bought me a playpen.
Dear Mum and Dad,
I love you so much,
You have always stayed with me
Even when it got tough.
You two are the ones who inspire me the most
And for that, I want to say thank you once more.

Isabella Yanez (11)
Deyes High School, Maghull

Family

I look up to my family,
Especially my grandad.
Even though he is dead,
I still look up to him.
He went through a lot in his childhood,
He was evacuated as a baby in World War 2.
He died last year due to cancer,
He was only 76.
But the good thing is that he had an amazing life
And a great personality.
I visit his grave every Sunday afternoon.

Kieran Burness (12)
Deyes High School, Maghull

All The Same

Although we are all the same we all have our own differences.
Whether you're a woman or a man,
Black or white, gay or straight we are all different
But instead of making fun or bullying someone for being different,
We should celebrate and accept people for it.
Because deep down we are all the same.
But we all feel the need to have approval from others.

Jamie Mccloy (11)
Deyes High School, Maghull

We All Love Christmas

The tree decorations sparkle in the night.
All the presents under the tree, what a beautiful sight.
Christmas songs on all day,
Playing with your new toys while you lie in bed,
Writing your Christmas list with a hot chocolate,
Looking outside to see the air filled with mist.
Unwrapping the presents on Christmas morning...
No one could be happier!

Lexi Taylor (12)
Deyes High School, Maghull

My Dad

My dad is the best,
I wouldn't trade him for the rest,
He's always trying his hardest,
Pushing me to try something but only once in a while,
He makes me feel better and always makes me smile,
He's very wise
And always has a surprise,
He supports me in every way,
I hope he never goes away,
He's the best in the world.

Albert Stewart (11)
Deyes High School, Maghull

Planet Earth

We are all connected, but some don't see,
That we are all joined genetically.

From the birds in the sky to the fish in the sea,
We are all as important as can be.

Planet Earth is where we live,
A paradise with much to give,
But we need Mother Nature to forgive
Or else all lifeforms we will outlive.

Mathew Hodgkiss (11)
Deyes High School, Maghull

Every Other Saturday

Every other Saturday is my best day off
and it's off to the match I go.
I love to take a walk around the Anfield road.
Me and my old pal Joe.
We love to see the lads with the red scarves on.
We love to hear Kopites roar
but I don't have to tell you that best of all
we love to see Liverpool score.

Jack Clayton (12)
Deyes High School, Maghull

We Are All Beautiful

We all have skin
Which we all must live in.
We don't all look the same
But there is no one to blame.
We laugh, we love, we cry
But all of us must fly.
Beauty is in the eye of the beholder
And doesn't change as we get older.
Always remember your worth
As it was given to you at birth.

Natasha Dix (12)
Deyes High School, Maghull

This Is Me

Models are thin.
Models are tall.
I am not like this at all.

I am small.
I wear glasses.
A model I will never be called.

Our beauty is not about
Being like them.
Our beauty is about being like us.

This is me.
That is that.
I am beautiful, just like that!

Penny Mulholland (11)
Deyes High School, Maghull

A World We Can Be

There is a world we can be,
No matter your gender or race,
Every man or woman, black or white,
We shall be free.
Old or young, you should not mix up your tongue
As you could make or break somebody else's day.
This is a world I believe we can be,
This is a world where we can be free!

Stephen Oyelowe
Deyes High School, Maghull

The Idenity

Identity... A word, right?
But what is the meaning of identity?
No discrimination of who they are or what they do.
You will always be different,
No one is correct or wrong,
Like trees have different appearances.
Harsh words thrown around will hurt anyone
No matter who they are.

Alex Ainscough (11)
Deyes High School, Maghull

Family

My family is one of the most important things in my life,
It would be horrible to lose them.
As well as being there for me
They are a big inspiration in my life,
They will do anything for me.
But you should never take it for granted.
There is nothing more important than family.

Harry Jones (12)
Deyes High School, Maghull

My Dog Makes Me, Me

You make me laugh
You make me smile
You make me cry
You make me, me.

You jump
You run
You sleep
You make me, me.

You fetch
You walk
You bark
You make me, me.

No matter what happens
You make me, me.

Owen Hamilton (11)
Deyes High School, Maghull

Racism Is Wrong

Roses are red
Violets are blue
We are all equal
Just like you
Racism is wrong
We should all sing
Our equality song
We should not have to fight
For our equal rights
We should all write
Why should we fight?
Let's all be bright.

Ethan Kendrick (12)
Deyes High School, Maghull

When I Play Football

I play centre midfield
When I got tackled, the doctors got me healed
When I don't score
I feel a burn in my core
When I score top bins
The opponents try to break my shins
When I do a great pass
The ball skims across the amazing green grass.

Haydn Norris (11)
Deyes High School, Maghull

The Environment

The environment cries every day
It's being destroyed in every way
The weather is constantly raging
Times are changing
The environment cries every day
It doesn't get a say
The sun is like a frying pan
Burning and giving a spicy tan.

Owain Madoc-Jones (11)
Deyes High School, Maghull

Mum

Dear Mum,
Thank you for everything,
for the kindest things you do.
Thank you for being there
and for putting me in front of you.
Thank you for supporting me
And showing me the way.
I wish I said it more,
I love you every day.

Harrison McGuiness (11)
Deyes High School, Maghull

My Family

My family, they protect me with all their might.
My family, they support me and make me feel bright.
My family, every time I'm down they brighten up my light.
My family, my family,
They are the definition of empowerment and empowering.

Charlie Doyle (12)
Deyes High School, Maghull

We Are All The Same

Whatever sex,
Whatever gender you may be,
We can all be happy,
We can all agree.
Whether you are a boy or a girl,
We are all the same,
Some people say we're different,
That's what some people claim.

Joseph Willis (12)
Deyes High School, Maghull

Family

Be thank **F** ul, always forgive
Sh **A** re, respect one another
Show co **M** passion, we make mistakes
Try th **I** ngs, say I love you
Laugh out **L** oud, be grateful
Know who **Y** ou are, be happy.

George Cox (12)
Deyes High School, Maghull

The Disappearance

They roar, then they snore,
They growl whilst they prowl.

Poachers stalk and hunt,
With knives not so blunt.

Numbers shrink in a blink,
Follow your instinct
Or species will be extinct.

Ava Boswell (11)
Deyes High School, Maghull

The Rich And Poor

Humans are humans,
No matter our wealth we all have good health.
Humans are humans,
We all have feelings, we are human beings.
Yes or no...
Are you poor or rich?
No matter what, humans are humans.

Faith Goodwin (11)
Deyes High School, Maghull

Everyone Is Perfect

Everyone is equal, no matter who they are,
The human race has come very far,
No matter your gender or race,
You all come first place,
No matter the day,
Everyone is perfect in their own way.

Zach Wooding (11)
Deyes High School, Maghull

Mockingbird

A flying canvas,
Spreading change,
A spectrum of emotions.

Fill the sky as it passes,
Silent and modest,
Hovering, as if by magic.

It cannot wave goodbye,
But it somehow does so without
An entrance or exit,

Without a message or a letter,
It searches for a distant land,
Which may not exist,

But the spirit lives inside
That tiny soul, which hides
In the shadows of others'

Foolishness. A silent killer, or
Detective, observing closely
As the trains go by,

Waiting on the washing
Lines, a fragrance of newly
Whitewashed fences,

Which it calls home;
Those minute legs
Which cling on as winter

Takes its toll. Eyes, which
Resemble the lakes of
A perfect land,

Branches which twist
And twist as the weight of
Veracity

Becomes too much to
Bear. Bullet holes left
From different eras,

Words said, and people
Ignored. It is easy to lie,
But it doesn't,

Instead sneering to
The bystander who makes
A long search for water,

Or food, to shelter the
Wounded mockingbird,
To find a sanctuary

For such a meaningless
Creature. But as you look
Twice, the flapping wings

Fall out of sight
Somewhere along
The line between

You and I,
Faintly flickering
In the dancing moonlight.

Radomir Stamatov (15)
Horizon Community College, Barnsley

Why Me?

The murmurs began.
Her breath tripped and stumbled
This... this was a mistake
Looks slashed holes in her silky skin
Her patience was running thin
Giggles and sniggers made her blood boil
As if infected with thick poison.
Tears demanded the sweet release from their emerald prisons
The words, *what's wrong with me?* were tattooed on her mind
What made me think I fit in...

Am I blind?

The mirror pulled and tugged at her parts
Its touch is more painful than being pierced with darts
Why me? she pondered.

Why do I jiggle when I walk?
Why does my voice crack when I talk?
Why does my laugh make people cringe?
Why when I'm emotional do I binge?
The reality is that the world is blind
The reality that you will find is that you are what you are...
And that is perfection.

Emma Rutter (12)
Horizon Community College, Barnsley

I Don't Understand

I don't understand why people refuse to put themselves in others' shoes,
Because that is the reason some people don't have shoes.
I don't understand why people go with the crowd,
Even if the crowd told them not to.
I don't understand smoking,
And why people can't see the lies beyond the mist of it.
I don't understand some education systems,
And I'm sure others don't either.
I don't understand discrimination,
And I don't even have to say why.

What I do understand is change,
Because that is the first step to understanding,
I do understand banding together,
Because that's how you make others understand.
I understand advocating,
For a better land.
I do understand resistance to the constant baiting,
Because the news feeds ignorance.
I know that others don't understand,
And I know my and their wants,
I understand unity,
To build a better community.

Where we are encouraged to do art,
Where little things don't break us apart.
Where peace is a constant state,
Where you don't have to always sit and wait.
Where you don't have to cheat and lie,
Where everyone understands why.

Elena Iordan (13)
Horizon Community College, Barnsley

Love

A powerful feeling, but not something
everyone has the privilege of seeing.
It may be abstract
maybe it's not,
but know this for certain: it leaves your heart
scrambled in knots.
Really it should
make you feel somewhat special.
And really it is
soft and gentle.
Sometimes love
will drown you in metres of mud.
And most of all, love
is really misjudged.
It can be described as many things:
Powerful, amazing, sensational.
But could love be
one of the deadly sins?

Maybe it could be that some are incapable of love,
or maybe it's that they hate the sight of doves.
Maybe it's that their heads aren't screwed on right,
or maybe their heads are screwed on too tight.
Whatever it is,
we know for certain

that not everyone can see
how great love can be
and maybe God did this to us on purpose.

Love cannot be around for all of eternity.
It's important to share what we have.
Love comes from us, internally.
So, show some courtesy,
and love those around you, and me.
Then you'll see that love, well,
love will always be some sort of mystery...

Darcie Stell (15)
Horizon Community College, Barnsley

Ridged

As we climb the ropes,
The ropes to death
We clamber slowly;
Awaiting our passing
Really? Why do we do it?

Our minds slowly tick
Tick like a bomb, as our companions
Believe, believe we should survive.

I approach the summit, here.
Here I am. Gusts lash me. Gusts slice me.
Gusts thrash our untenanted minds.
Sludge hinders us, we're an empty threat
Just like our minds, unfelt and missed.

We are all unphased, or so it seems,
Scourged are our heads.
Time gradually ticks.

The ridge scorched us;
There is no sun.
A battle that has lasted forever,
Ten minutes since we began.
Who is left?

Continuously ticking, time does so,
An explosion is pending:
Worst has not been done.

Machine guns blast;
Ahead of us, we become the past
Yet we still charge forward, negligent of the future.
Whistles sliver the air, blare our ears.
Outlay a medic, no assistance remaining in him.

The shroud of ticking pursues, yet now much more oppressive.
The charge is primed, doom besieges us, for we
Are ridged...

Bang!

Charlie Senior
Horizon Community College, Barnsley

Epoch

Epoch, ever near time yet unspaced,
Death's not here, yet Epoch,
Unresumed, illogical to see,
My soul not my own and yet just a piece,
Brooken down by damned puppet strings,
A broken gear upon a complex apparatus.

So does this have to be?
Like wedding bells in an empty church,
Like blank shore in a blackened boat,
Like an empty boat in a loved town,
Like a lost submarine near the Mariana Trench,
Like a bottle of its deepest sorrows?

No? Well then my friend,
A darkened sky may draw near,
So if darkest lights lead to bright skies.
A closed case, my friend, let me say
What! Broken tines, dark and light -
Remain unevoked - my friend! After all -
No solutions, no darkness can hide
Speaking may stutter -
But so may silence

Rest down, nothing needed,
No more stress, no more conditions,
Please do not fear for the dark does not cry,

No story - no story, no little time,
For now you can rest -
For now you can rest -
No work left behind.

Nothing untrue in divide.

Adam Oliver
Horizon Community College, Barnsley

If I Was A God What Would I Do?

I would cover myself in a tempest that no one could hope to clear
I would strike an almighty bolt of lightning to all my enemies that created all the anger inside of me
I was welcomed to Olympus with all my family and friends
Happy forevermore... but there is one thing, I wonder, who am I or what am I?

I look inside my head and find a blizzard not only I can make disappear
When I am with my family and friends all this fear fades away
When I strike my thunder to the realm below all the people cower in fear and beg for mercy
All I really want is for people to trust me and treat me how they'd like to be treated themselves.

Years have passed in the world below but in my head I am just falling deeper into an abyss, with no end in sight
People call me a myth, a deity, omnipotent, but I am just a person with an unnatural ability
I will not be called a monster, a god, ruler of Olympus
I am who I want to be, not what people want me to be.

I am limitless and will be remembered by the people who got to know me...
The real me.

Isaac-Jae Jackson
Horizon Community College, Barnsley

Darkness

I can see that you're hurting
Your heart has been wronged
And I know you are doing your best
To stay strong.

I want to let someone know
I will never let them go
And I will stay by their side
Until sorrow is gone.

Even if they don't believe me
Happiness can come their way
For nothing in this world
Was ever meant to stay.

Until then I can lend you my shoulder
So you can let your tears fall
While I banish all the shadows
That has your heart under control.

I won't turn away
When you show me your scars
I can accept them all
Just like I do with your bright smiles.

That's why I beg
Never hide your pain from my sight

I am here to help your burden
And keep you company
Until you feel alright.

Can I really see you hurting?
Can I see you hurting?
Can I see future happiness?
Can I lend a shoulder?
Can I keep you company?

Can I get out of the darkness?

Kate Ledger (14)
Horizon Community College, Barnsley

Shiver

Burnt, killed off and bleeding,
Dropping to the floor without feeling,
Like being shot with a bullet but you're still breathing,
Betrayed by the one that helped you,
Now you're out on the floor,
Frozen.

They held out the gold but dropped it before your hands,
Now you're shivering and stuck,
Paranoia has struck,
As you lay on the street failing,
Can you trust?

Undeniable lights flash before your eyes,
Is this the way you die?
Your fighting effort... gone,
And as you reach for peace,
The victory you need to live and breathe,
You are stepped on for the final time,
Rendering your consciousness gone,

So you're left to die on the streets you walked on...

Shivering.

Justin Howlett
Horizon Community College, Barnsley

Determination

It's about reaching for the stars and landing on the moon,
Rather than reaching for the moon and being stranded in space,
Not knowing what to do.

It's about knowing what you want to do and doing it
Instead of waiting for someone to do it for you
Or before you.

It's about you knowing your potential
And matching that up with your priorities and your possibilities.

Be optimistic because you never know
Some of your dreams might just come true
Because it motivates you
There isn't much that can stop you.

There will be some challenges on the way
Small and big, some that you won't even imagine tackling,
But if you don't try, you'll never know what might have happened.

Nathaniel Wathey (14)
Horizon Community College, Barnsley

Soldier's Trauma

Disassociating from sad reality
Falling away slowly
From life
From themselves
From all that is good
And all that once mattered

Memories are the only thing that remain
Images haunt the mind all day
All night.
Nothing drowns them out.
The silence - deafening
The voices of those who weren't so lucky
Playing non-stop.

They are not the same
The lovers, they came back after war
Are no longer with the person with whom they fell in love
Their children are the children of strangers
They will never be the same.

Serenity is on the periphery
If only pain could halt for a day
A moment even
But it won't
And if it did
How pleasant could that be?

Rebekah Carrington (14)
Horizon Community College, Barnsley

Snow: The Last Thing I Ever See

It's the calm before the storm, the dark before the dawn
Our bodies exhausted, soaked and muddy
The smoke-filled sky crying white as shots are fired for one last time.
I hear three shots fired, one hitting the metal fence behind me,
Another hitting the ground beneath me.
The last one lost? Or so I thought.
An immense burning in my chest, awakening suddenly.
The last bullet impaled into my chest.
I feel myself letting go, as if I'm disconnecting from the world
The snow being the last thing I ever see,
I said my final goodbye before I feel my heartbeat one last time.
I feel myself taking my last breath
I feel myself leaving the physical world.
Darkness begins to paint over my eyes.
Gone.

Faith Lumb (15)
Horizon Community College, Barnsley

Poisonous Words

Like poison
The venom of your words
Slithered its way into my self-worth
It ran through my veins
Feeling nothing but pain

My self-worth
Slipping away
I begged it to stay
As it walked away

They cut deeper than a knife
Cutting their way into the last bit of hope
Did you think?
Did you care?
Probably not, but it wasn't fair.

They pull at my hair
Tug at my head
Nothing can help, not even my bed
Do you know what they do to my head?

Lost in thoughts, the venom of your words
That no one else heard
Finally left my head
When my self-worth was found dead

Poisonous words
Are all I that I heard.

Kirstie Bennett (14)
Horizon Community College, Barnsley

Now Everybody Knows

Raindrops into the deepest of oceans
Water doesn't have an expiration date,
But I do.

A metal hope gleams at the end of the fresh white bed
A fear of falling under
A chance at freedom
Is what I have.

My chest gasps of air
But I don't
A need drowns me, a want consumes me
So I listen.

If you don't succeed try, try again
A rule I follow
Something I live by
But it didn't work.

Hidden like a drop of rain in the vastest ocean
The truth of what happened
Nobody knows...
But I do.

I swam to the top
Clawed above the seas
Reached above the trauma
Now everybody knows.

Holly Casken (14)
Horizon Community College, Barnsley

Dear Future Me

Dear future me,
Be whoever you wanna be,
An engineer, a technician,
I will go on a mission
To be that better person
We always wanted to be.

I will spend more time with the person I love
Because one day they may be looking down from above.
I want to make them proud
And be the king of the crowd.

I want people to love me for me - for who I am
I will stand up and be different from everyone else.

I am limitless.

I will ignore the negativity
And spread the happiness
I will work hard
And make my dreams come true
Because if you only believe
You can succeed too.

Harry Tordoff (14)
Horizon Community College, Barnsley

If I Were The Prime Minister...

If I were the prime minister
I would do something sinister
It would become very fair
For the people who care.

Donate for trees
Hashtag: Save The Bees
Lower those fees
That's what I'd do
If I were the prime minister.

If I were the prime minister
I would do something sinister
It would become very fair
For the people who care.

Don't ruin our world
We only have one
Just look what you've become
This is what I'd do
If I were the prime minister.

Vote for a better leader
Who can fix this

With some cement and bricks
If I were the leader I would fix this.

Beau Burrows (11)
Horizon Community College, Barnsley

Dear My Past Self

Dear my past self,
I couldn't reach the highest shelf,
I couldn't be the best,
I always needed rest.

Dear my past self,
No trophies on my shelf,
My best friend betrayed me,
I couldn't really be me.

Dear my past self,
I didn't look after myself,
I need to focus on my future,
With one too many computers.

Dear my future self,
Ten trophies on my shelf,
I'm currently the best,
I'll always have some rest.

Dear my future self,
I can reach the highest shelf,
I have so many best friends,
Our friendship will never end!

Oliver Morgan (11)
Horizon Community College, Barnsley

I Want To Feel Alive

I want to go on a road trip someday,
Alone or with someone I love.
I want to get away,
Explore places,
Sleep in the car,
Stop a lot just to admire the view,
Visit museums and try out coffee shops,
Listen to my favourite albums whilst driving,
Have a polaroid camera,
Take pretty pictures of the sunrise,
Take pictures of myself,
Run through a forest,
Chase fog,
Chase the sun,
Spend hours on a field making flower crowns,
Feel the wind in my hair,
Buy souvenirs,
Meet people,
Take time to observe,
I want to make memories.
I want to feel alive.

Lilly Sephton (13)
Horizon Community College, Barnsley

Believe And Achieve

B elieve in your dreams
E veryone can have dreams.
L ove yourself as much as you love anyone else.
I ndividually unique.
E xactly the same but different dreams and hopes.
V ery much the same.
E veryone has dreams

A nd they can be achieved.
N ever give up.
D ream and dream

A nd never give up.
C onfidence,
H appiness and hope
I s the key to our goals.
E veryone is the same.
V ery much the same.
E veryone has dreams, which we can achieve.

Lily Hobbs
Horizon Community College, Barnsley

Willy The Fly

Oh dear fly,
you didn't have to die,
you could have lived a life,
a child, a husband, a wife.

I hope the afterlife treats you nice,
even if you looked like you were on 'spice',
I loved how you looked,
it made my eyes hooked.

Your best friend 'Bee' crying outside the window,
he'll never be able to see you again though.
We're all in the grieving process,
because we loved you the mostest.

Oh Willy the fly, you will be missed,
even if you made everyone p*****.

RIP Willy.

Izzy Gardham (13)
Horizon Community College, Barnsley

Time To Change

Transport,
Farming,
Fashion,
Breathing out CO_2.
Fossil fuels really are the worst.
The cutting down of all our trees,
Not breathing in CO_2.
The planet has got hotter,
There's time to stop the rise.
Avoid the point of no return,
When the planet is beyond repair.

People need to come together,
There's still time to reverse what's been done.
If we come together, our world will have a future,
As now it is the time of change.

Elliot D E Clarke (13)
Horizon Community College, Barnsley

Anxiety

The brain works in strange ways,
Telling you you can't do it and to turn the other way.
What you do isn't good enough,
These things are tough.
Chaos around you but a prison in your mind,
But it's time, you're not blind, you know your stuff.
The voice in your head is way too loud,
Feeling like you're trapped in a crowd.
Drowning in the sea, but take a breath, do not flee.
Raise your voice, stand up tall, this wave of stress will one day fall.

Bryony Jennings
Horizon Community College, Barnsley

Dear Future Self

Dear future self,
I have one request,
Be confident
And try your best.

Dear future self,
I have one thing to say,
Be kind
And smile at the end of every day.

Dear future self,
Another request,
Respect your friends and family
And remember to welcome every guest.

Oh, and one last thing,
Remember you are amazing,
Be confident and shimmer in the spotlight as the years go by,
Never forget to be yourself.

Jessica Gosling (11)
Horizon Community College, Barnsley

Empowered

Be yourself, don't be frightened
To show who you are.
Keep the people close to you, they are
Like a permanent bold piece of art.

People make all the knots disappear
And make you stable.
We are unique, no one's normal,
You are admirable don't forget that.

You're like the sun awakening in the morning,
Bright and ecstatic.
Learn to love yourself.

Don't be in the dim,
Be in the luminous.

Isabella Wilby (12)
Horizon Community College, Barnsley

Do You...

Do you still gaze upon the pictures that you drew
Or talk to all those people, those people you once knew?
Do you still chase after things
Or go for walks, besides in spring
Or sing and dance all day long?
Do you imagine people cheering you on?
Do you sit outside and stare at the sky?
Do you watch the birds fly by?

But why? Why bother?

After all, it's all just a dream.

This world is not at all what it seems.

Jasmine Burton (13)
Horizon Community College, Barnsley

Aeternum

It lingers
It lays
It follows you every day
It's like embroidery for the skin
The type that causes a piercing pain
A pain that will last forever
Haunting like a caliginous shadow
All of this betrayal
All of this regret
It's like a jail
An iron fist that holds you in
An empty void that breaks your will
What can I say?
This tattoo will hold you from going your own way.

Carla Macoviciuc
Horizon Community College, Barnsley

A Problem

A problem can come
In many ways and forms
Like a problem with
My homework or with
The way I look?

A problem forms another
Until it creates a chain
Of problems one
After another.
When will it
Ever change?

A problem will be
A problem if you
Create it but
One day or maybe
One week the
Problem will be

A problem that
Is fixed.

Senuli Perera (12)
Horizon Community College, Barnsley

The Power Of Love

Envy. Envy. Envy.
Envy individuality,
Envy others,
Envy society,
Envy the world.
Envy. Envy. Envy.

We need change.
We cannot have it instantly.
We need to persevere.
We must lose our everlasting fear
And step into reality.

Love. Love. Love.
Love individuality,
Love others,
Love society,
Love the world.
Love. Love. Love.

Molly Holmes
Horizon Community College, Barnsley

Toxic Masculinity

When was the last time you cried?
Was it today? Yesterday? Or forever ago?
Which one was it?

When was the last time you spoke out?
Was it today? Yesterday? Or forever ago?
Which one was it?

When was the last time you were hurt?
Was it today? Yesterday? Or forever ago?
Which one... was it?

Ashton Wilkinson (15)
Horizon Community College, Barnsley

English

English is the gateway to success,
English is the open path to happiness,
English is the next generation.

The new era to poems, writing and spelling,
English is one of a kind,
English changes our minds.

Aaron Shah
Horizon Community College, Barnsley

Reflection

Love shows the beauty on the inside,
Love shows you what other people see,
I like to dance and sing in front of love,
Love reflects what is in front of you,
And hurts more than you can ever know.

Megan Lowes
Horizon Community College, Barnsley

A Bath Of Sunlight

Envy is a bath of sunlight,
Flowing out of the sky,
Washing off the day with a bath,
Slowly rising above and over.

Lily Graham (15)
Horizon Community College, Barnsley

To My Past, Present And Future

My dear past,
I beg thee, with the force of lions,
With the screams of a banshee,
To stop.
Put simply to stop constantly thinking of
actions, of words, of people, of places
And stop,
Don't lie awake at the crack of dawn,
Don't schedule the night, for the night is no time for thinking
and reconciliation of the mind.
For each tear and sob shan't be timed
For the names you loved and hated sometimes
Shan't be silently screamed or mimed,
Don't waste the ebony deity's time
With disintegrating the memories of mine
Convincing yourself with carefully woven lies
For in the fantasy of memory is where an emotionally
unstable beast lies.

To you my dear present,
To me now,
I have five words for you,
You have let me down.

My future,
Your rough, calloused hands hold
Beginnings, endings and unfortunately middles.
Is my path paved with shattered glass?
Am I porcelain? Am I a mirror laced with regret?
Are your nights drowned in tears?
Your days deprived of true emotion?
Are you with a child?
A child of resentment, of defeat?
Are your eyes the moon, a milky, lifeless haze?
Does your time, money and happiness lie in a hastily ending material possession?
Are you isolated in a barbed-wire fence of your aggression?
Does jewellery of jealousy or empathy adorn your soul?
As my words are soon silenced by a writing end
I can't resist to wonder...
Are you there or are you a shadow?
A shell of a person, trapped in another's memory.
Do you die in your sleep or...
Shall my wristed be stained crimson by the fall of night?

Emaan Anwar (11)
Our Lady & St Bede Catholic Academy, Stockton-On-Tees

Memories

People can drag you back,
Friends can keep you down,
Family can also tackle you to the ground
Or they can do the complete opposite.
They can give you a lift,
They can help you up,
They can protect you no matter what.
Whatever happens,
They are your memories now
As solid as a brick wall.
Some are forgotten,
Some are still with you,
All your life.
When you look back on your memories,
You could feel happiness,
You could feel sadness,
You could feel guiltiness,
You could feel anger,
You could feel fear,
To be honest the list goes on.
But remember,
The precious memories of yours will be locked away
In a special vault in your heart,
Letting nothing but yourself see them,
And the painful ones will go in the recycling bin

To be forgotten and to be renewed into a new
Joyful, exciting, wonderful memory.
However...
If you can't manage to remember your memories
Of the past,
Try and find something old and precious
That belongs to you,
It could be a teddy,
It could be a toy plane,
It could be an empty vase,
It could even be a glittering crystal that is a star
In your eyes,
And remember this,
There will always be something
Valuable, precious, beaming
That is packed with gorgeous memories.
And one last thing...
A painting is worth thousands
But a memory is priceless.
Life is short
But memories make it massive.
When you say goodbye to the Earth
Leave with memories not dreams.

Codrin Catana (11)
Our Lady & St Bede Catholic Academy, Stockton-On-Tees

The Real Me

After years of struggles, I thought I was free,
Now, as I stare into the mirror, and what do I see?
My greatest fear, which is buried deep inside me,
Years of trying,
Screaming for help,
Now I feel like crying,
Remembering my past pain,
My head feels like a raging storm,
All these thoughts begin to form,
Twisting and turning,
They all started to swarm.
I don't want to face this again,
Even though I know what to do,
Perhaps I'll just try to pray, "Our Lord, Amen,"
I can't do this again with all I had to go through.

Perhaps this time will be better,
For this time I have hope,
I won't give up,
I won't just roll up in a ball like a sweater,
I will no longer hide like I'm tied in a rope.

I'm not saying this won't be hard,
I'm not saying this won't be a struggle,
I'm not saying it will be a breeze,
Nor will I do this with ease,

But I refuse to go down this road again,
At least not like last time,
This time, I will be just fine.

Maybe I have another chance,
Just one more chance to save myself,
I will get up,
I will stand up,
Not one more day shall I suffer,
Just for approval of another.

Now, once again, I stare in that mirror,
Now, what do I see?
My greatest quality,
The real me.

Milo Knowles (13)
Our Lady & St Bede Catholic Academy, Stockton-On-Tees

Change

Nobody wants to grow up.
Nobody wants to move away.
Nobody wants to leave behind the happiness of childhood.
Nobody wants to change.
Nobody wants to say goodbye to the times before.
Nobody wants to say goodbye to an easy life.
But that's how it goes...
You grow up, you change, you say goodbye.
Nothing can stay the same forever.

I used to hope that my life wouldn't change.
I used to hope I would always have the same friends.
That I would always have that bond with the people that I love.
I always hoped no one would ever leave me.
But over the years I have come to terms with the reality that life will change.
Life will be different.

You will lose people, but you will also gain incredible people.
And they are the ones you have to hold onto.
They are the ones that matter.
Because, in the long run, they are the people that have been there through the hard times.
They are the people who really know how to care about you.

So keep those people close, because when you lose them, and it is too late, you will regret it.
Cherish the people you love.
Keep them close.
Keep them in your heart.
Never forget about the times spent with anyone.
Because it is the memories that matter.
Even if everything has changed.

Hayley Paskin-Bell (14)
Our Lady & St Bede Catholic Academy, Stockton-On-Tees

Injustice

The place we call home is a fragile place
Through people to creatures to problems we face
Continuous questions of 'what if' or 'why'
Cause fear, pain and force us to hide
We feel injustice.

From finding yourself in fields of white
Longing bright colour, not equality fights
Searching for purpose, looking for light
Instead of standing and enjoying your unique little life
We see injustice.

But not just for us, but the environment too
The endless battle of 'the right thing to do'
Whilst some blame their friends and others confess
Some of them pause to speak out and protest
We smell injustice.

People may stay hidden in a dark empty space
As they try to catch up to society's pace
They struggle to fit, to survive on their own
So, we need to check up on them, preventing their lone
We taste injustice.

Finally, we all look back
We look and address the equality we lack

Notice the people we watch walk by
As we take deep breaths and look at the sky
We can change injustice.

Emily Saint (14)
Our Lady & St Bede Catholic Academy, Stockton-On-Tees

Climate Change

Climate change
It's a current situation that affects everyone
And if not changed now there will be nowhere to run
Greta has told us we need to go green
To save our land for future teens.

Turning your light off when not in the room
To prevent the creation of gases and fumes
Turning your tap off when not brushing your teeth
To help stop killing the coral reef.

Pandas are down to a few
Polar bears are even suffering too
Plastics are choking wildlife until it dies
Don't say you haven't contributed, I know it's a lie.

If you love the trees that provide us with life
You should strive to help them and stop carving them with a knife
If you love the land we call home
You should care for it, like when you brush your hair with a comb.

Climate change is a current issue
Our home should be treated with care
And not just flung around like a tissue.

Raine Longstaff (14)
Our Lady & St Bede Catholic Academy, Stockton-On-Tees

Autism

People are created different,
People are built different,
People are judged for their conditions,
People are stereotyped and given a title.
People are like a jigsaw.
People can be a puzzle sometimes.
People are belittled,
Bullied,
Beaten,
Because they think they are not smart or normal.
But there are people who rise from this oppression,
There are people who help stop this oppression,
There are people who back up those who are oppressed.
There are people who make a difference by proving that a book should never be judged by its cover,
Who believe that a disability is not a disability but a different ability,
Who protect and defend all who are oppressed and taken advantage of.
People who help all who are different,
People who protect all who are different,
People who try to make them a complete puzzle.

John Nicholson
Our Lady & St Bede Catholic Academy, Stockton-On-Tees

The Fire

A ferocious fire screams loud and clear,
'Children of the future do not fear
Because, behold, your justice is near'
They set a flame of hope in me.

The smoke they release is oh so sweet,
Many flames of light, they wave and greet
Their raging force and thunder feet -
Set a flame of hope in me.

Rainwater falls from enemies' eyes
They ignore our loud and painful cries
We're not extinguished, instead we rise -
They set a flame of hope in me.

Each amber flame, so young, so old
Has a burning story to be told
Their skin empowered, richer than gold -
They set a flame of hope in me...

And perhaps this ferocious fire
Will set us free.

Caroline Cummings (14)
Our Lady & St Bede Catholic Academy, Stockton-On-Tees

Everyone's Game

The main problem in the beautiful game today is racism.

At the Euros it was at its peak,
Racist fans filling our seats.

The Saka miss was the worst,
'Supporters' with insults ready and rehearsed.

But they came back, Sterling and Saka, back to performing,
However Rashford and Sancho didn't hit the mark,
Taking all the racism to heart.

A lot of words and messages were sent their way,
Keyboard warriors think they're safe,
But still get exposed for their hate.

At the end of the day we're all the same,
Skin colour and race shouldn't change the way we treat one another.

Because one thing unites us all,
The beautiful game.

Ashton Edwards (15)
Our Lady & St Bede Catholic Academy, Stockton-On-Tees

Hate Is Toxic

In this world not everybody has rights
Most of the time people get into fights
Negativity spreads like toxic waste
Then people start hating at a sudden pace.

The environment's in danger
So it's getting quite major
But we can't get a quick enough solution
So things are starting like pollution.

Now let's move onto a positive side
Where things are taking a different ride
We are a different generation
Which means we aren't taking a vacation.

We are gonna fight for our rights
Even if it takes us many days and nights
We are gonna help the Earth which is in need
And we will succeed.

Poppy Kelly (11)
Our Lady & St Bede Catholic Academy, Stockton-On-Tees

Where You Are

You sit alone, again.
Every day seems to be the same.
You are told you aren't on your own,
But deep inside you know.
You know that they have all of your control,
But you feel so small and you know they know.
But when you meet the younger you,
Look them in the eyes
And tell them the truth.
Let them know that their one mean word
Could never equate to the million you're worth.
Tell them that you made it,
And that you're happy.
Because without your struggle
You wouldn't be where you are
So to those demons who made you feel alone,
It gets better.
Look at where you are now.

Ellie Blackburn (15)
Our Lady & St Bede Catholic Academy, Stockton-On-Tees

The Person Who Inspires Me

You gave me my name, you gave me hope,
You gave me strength, you helped me with my weaknesses,
And all I want to say is thank you very much.

You gave me my power when I was weak,
You helped me with my problems when I was stuck,
And all I want to say is thank you very much.

You gave me a place to stay,
You helped me sleep when I could not rest,
You gave me advice in life and it always helped,
And for that, I want to say thank you very much.

You are and will always be, the one person who inspired me,
I am very grateful and happy,
And all I want to say is thank you very much.

Muhammad Ayaan Waseem (11)
Our Lady & St Bede Catholic Academy, Stockton-On-Tees

Distance

We had our laughs, we had our cries
Within a second we were strangers again
What went wrong, was it me? Or was it he?

Happiness quickly turned into darkness, putting
Me into a dark place. A hole that I dug long ago.
A stormy night that turned into a sunny day,
It got worse before it got better.

It finally changed. The storm clouds have
Disappeared. He made me have a purpose, he made
Me feel confident within myself. The pain was
Gone as his eyes distracted me from reality.

Before I was broken. And she is a distant memory
That is long forgotten.

Jessica Chesser (15)
Our Lady & St Bede Catholic Academy, Stockton-On-Tees

The Juicy And Magical Apple

Whose apple is that? I think I know.
Its owner is quite happy though.
Full of joy like a vivid rainbow,
I watch him laugh. I cry hello.

He gives his apple a shake,
And laughs until his belly aches.
The only other sound's the break,
Of distant waves and birds awake.

The apple is juicy, magical and deep,
But he has promises to keep,
After cake and lots of sleep,
Sweet dreams come to him cheap.

He rises from his gentle bed,
With thoughts of kittens in his head,
He eats his jam with lots of bread,
Ready for the day ahead.

Calin Ionita (11)
Our Lady & St Bede Catholic Academy, Stockton-On-Tees

Speak Out

Be proud! Speak out! Never doubt!
You were made to stand and be bold,
You weren't made to fit the mould.
Stand strong and don't let go of the people you know.
Shout out as loud as you can for what you believe.
Be what you are, let yourself be free.
Forget your worries and be the best you can be.
Be proud of yourself for who you are.
You will always be special in your own way.
Give your say every day for the people you love,
Your life will rise and your say will never die!

Oscar Allan (11)
Our Lady & St Bede Catholic Academy, Stockton-On-Tees

Fight For Females

Degrading, discriminating, damaging,
All for the fight of empowering.
A hierarchy of slobs,
Forming angry female mobs.
Suffering and sacrifice for the identity of she,
These are the women I aspire to be.

Those women shackled to the fence
Each link screaming injustice,
With every man still screaming, "Trust us!"
How could we trust
When we see the look of anger and disgust.

All they wanted was a vote
Of which each man would gladly gloat.

Evie Dixon (14)
Our Lady & St Bede Catholic Academy, Stockton-On-Tees

Polar Bears

Polar bears and koalas, almost extinct.
How can we prevent this from happening?
Let's make the future brighter.

Wildfires destroying creatures' habitats
And animals not knowing what to do.
What are we going to do to stop this from happening?

Polar bears, struggling to find food.
Now you can see them looking on the streets for their dinner.
How can we help?

Annabelle McGlade (11)
Our Lady & St Bede Catholic Academy, Stockton-On-Tees

Make A Change

Today could be the day that you change the world.
Today could be the day that mistakes are made.
The world is the limit
But some people just do not know when to stop.
The time is going faster,
Plastic pollution, black lives matter.
Please people, stop.
You're ruining the planet,
Littering is a bad habit.

Noah Dixon (11)
Our Lady & St Bede Catholic Academy, Stockton-On-Tees

Trapped

Depression leaves a stain
It leaves an imprint on your brain
Anything can bring you pain
All your happiness goes down the drain
The tears in your eyes you can't contain
What's overwhelming is the permanent rain
Not knowing if tomorrow you'll still be sane
But depression is not your name.

Alice O'Connor (12)
Our Lady & St Bede Catholic Academy, Stockton-On-Tees

Deep Below

Deep, deep, deep in the dark below
There was a long and loud bellow.
It flew by like a bird in the sky
A whale looking for its dinner.
The water rushed like a floor being brushed
And it disappeared,
Deep, deep below.

Harry Woodcock (11)
Our Lady & St Bede Catholic Academy, Stockton-On-Tees

Proud

H urt feelings aren't funny
O pen stares are seen
M any jokes are made
O nly a different love
P laying someone else
H umans, we are still humans
O nly human, we should be proud
B eing ourselves shouldn't be feared
I am not changing for you
A ncient beliefs should be forgotten

I shouldn't be afraid of who I am
S houldn't hide who I love

W ho I am isn't wrong
R ebels are what we'll be
O nly I decide who I am
N o one should feel alone
G o out and there and be brave, for you are you and you are proud.

Leonna Roberts (13)
St Cenydd Community School, Trecenydd

Why Should She Feel Different

She goes to school every day,
She meets her friends by the local corner shop,
She walks up to her friends but no one notices she's even there,
She looks at them with their golden hair and big eyes,
She looks down at her hair, her eyes, her lips and glasses,
She hears them talking about all the boys they are texting,
She looks down at her phone to see nothing,
She looks at her recent texts, but the only texts there are from her mum and dad,
She thinks to herself, *Why do I feel different?*
She goes through the day with her mask up to her nose, scared to show her face,
By why should she feel different when she's just being herself?
Why should she feel left out when no one wants to talk to her?
Why should she feel insecure, even though all her features are just as beautiful as her friends'?
Why should she feel different, just because she doesn't text or even like boys?
Why should she feel different?

She's beautiful,
She's smart,
She's kind,
So why should she feel different?

Lily Owen (13)
St Cenydd Community School, Trecenydd

Positive Mindset

Follow dreams, show people what you're made of,
Try your best, aim to be the best version of yourself.
Want to become a professional rugby player?
Put your mind to it,
become that person you want to be.
Want to be a nurse, dentist, doctor?
Challenge yourself, try to become that person.
Keep your mindset positive.
Want to make a difference in this world?
Be kind, be helpful, be respectful.
Put yourself in someone else's shoes,
always be kind,
You never know what someone is going through.
Stop stereotyping,
let people be who they want to be.
Everyone's different,
if everyone was the same,
life would be boring.

Robyn Hall (13)
St Cenydd Community School, Trecenydd

The Future

What will the future be?
Tomorrow is the past, tomorrow is the future.
Will I be a writer next week or next year?
Or will I be a plumber tomorrow?
What will the future be?
Yesterday I was a gardener, today I was a student, but tomorrow
I might be a scientist or a mathematician or a historian.
What will the future be?
Tomorrow I might want to get an A in Maths or an A in Science.
What you choose will shape your future.
Your teacher doesn't make your future.
Your family, loved ones, classmates, or your friends at work, don't make your future.
You make your future.
What will the future be?

James Clark (13)
St Cenydd Community School, Trecenydd

No One

E mpowered: what does it mean?
M any are believing what they see on a screen
P eople will hate you if you're not a certain weight
O r because you're black, brown, or just not straight
W hy should we feel like we have to hide?
E veryone deserves some power in their stride
R aces don't just end after one person has won
E very sky has a sun
D on't dare change for anyone, you are not a 'no one'.

Olivia Coghlan (14)
St Cenydd Community School, Trecenydd

Dear Younger Me

Dear younger me,
I hope soon you will be able to see
how much you will turn out to be.
Like a peach, so young and sweet.
One day, you might meet
somebody with handwriting so neat,
it might remind you of future me.
Maybe someday you'll like peas,
maybe you'll grow up to save the bees,
maybe you will sail the seas.
Or maybe you'll just be me,
or you
and you'll find something to do
and someone to be.

Caitlyn Ford (13)
St Cenydd Community School, Trecenydd

Life Is Worth It

A lot of people think life sucks
and they just want to end it all.
You were created to live.
You have people who care.
Life, it's not worth giving it up,
life always has hard times.
Even when you think you have lost everything,
maybe tell a teacher
or a friend
or at least someone you trust.
I hope you don't give up,
trust me,
life is worth it!

Ash Evans (14)
St Cenydd Community School, Trecenydd

Spare Me

Nothing's real,
I can't feel,
I want to heal,
I'm forced to kneel,
Spare my soul,
Count me out,
I see the sun,
From inside out,
Help me, God,
Speak the truth,
Will I make it
Day or night?

Joshua Fouweather (13)
St Cenydd Community School, Trecenydd

The Earth Is Dying, Nobody Knows

The leaves dance majestically in the calm breeze,
Over yonder, where the jagged ice peaks freeze,
Flowers dancing, blossom and bloom,
Trees sleeping soundly under the luminous moon,
The Earth is bright, everything grows.

Trees once happy, begin to fade,
The Earth is beginning to crumble because of what we made,
Great beasts are dying, all hope is lost,
To satisfy our greed, to fill our homes, was it worth it? What did it cost?
The Earth is dying, nobody knows.

What have we done to our once home?
In the blazing heat, all humans moan,
First, it was fine, we didn't need to worry,
However, only now will we be sorry,
The Earth is dead, we have no place to go.

Rhys Tadhunter (12), Jay & Charlie
St George's CE School, Gravesend

Perfect

You're perfect,
Any size, shape, or form,
No need to change or transform,
Stay the way you are,
You're a star.

Your teeth may be yellow,
Too shy to say hello,
We are all different,
However, all magnificent.

You may be tall,
You may be small,
You're still really cool,
It doesn't matter at all.

You may have greasy hair,
That you just can't bear,
Your skin may be rough,
You're still amazingly tough.

Everyone is unique,
No one is weak,
Always accept,
You are perfect.

Scarlett Trott (11)
St George's CE School, Gravesend

Winter Days

Winter days are every year,
They are what I admire.
Sitting down in the living room,
Playing by the fire.
Sipping hot chocolate, playing in the snow,
But when it turns to mush, the fun goes.
Sadness is short-lasting,
Because then, again, it starts snowing!
People running back outside,
Others going in to hide.
Crisp-thin snowflakes land on tongues,
Carollers singing cheerful songs.
Then, the best holiday of the year,
Christmas time, let's spread some cheer,
The very next year goes quickly.

James Allison (11)
St George's CE School, Gravesend

Fallen Soldiers

Fallen soldiers,
Scattered all over the Earth's floor,
There was one, two, three and four.
Too many to count for you or me,
Splayed out further than the eye can see.
The last thing that matters now is health,
Bodies align like books on a shelf.

Fallen soldiers,
with cuts and bruises.
Oh, but the blood just oozes.
There was no way out,
All you could do was shout.
The tears, the fears,
It went on for years.
Oh, this time was rotten,
Gone but never forgotten,
Fallen soldiers.

Tyler Parker (15)
St George's CE School, Gravesend

Empowered

She felt the power surging through her veins,
She felt no sorrow, guilt, or pain,
The friendships she'd formed disappeared, long gone,
It was fake, fraud all along,
Blinded by greed, power and more,
She stole their powers and grew more and more,
Evil, she was evil to the core,
She cackled as her friends fell to the floor,
They lay limp, weak and bruised,
She knew with this power she'd never lose,
She felt empowered, strong and bold,
As her malicious eyes glared, distant and cold.

Mercedes Asamoah-Brown (13)
St George's CE School, Gravesend

My Universe

My universe's eyes are the deep blue midnight sky
Her hair is as golden as the sun and stars
Her cheeks are as rosy as Mars
When she speaks, it's like hearing the sweet melodies of the heavens
She moves like a beautiful goddess
Her heart and soul are as pure as fluffy white clouds
Her skin is as fair as snow
Her hands as soft as wool
My universe holds all of my heart
My universe holds the energy to my life.

Sienna Dalton (13)
St George's CE School, Gravesend

Embrace

Silently stalking, staring, strife,
Pain and sadness, hearts to the knife.
The sun's shimmer, the moon's luminous glow,
Embrace the darkness, or reap what you sow.

The morning robin, the nightly crow,
Own the futility or reap what you sow.
Frightfully falling, failure, defiance,
The only song worth singing is silence.
Embrace, embrace the darkness.

Nathan Bains (12)
St George's CE School, Gravesend

I Would Rather

I would rather have my feet sinking in the sand
than have my phone always in my hand.
The loud music of people in the street
but I'm sat here in the heat.
Leaving my social life behind
and having the feeling of being captured, rewind.
Although the journey is long
and the road is bumpy,
there is a plan for people
who need an extra hand.

Sahil Somani (13)
St George's CE School, Gravesend

Darkness

Darkness is fear,
We hope for light but it doesn't appear,
It's nowhere near,
This is the life I live in fear,
Horror is the only thing I can hear,
Listen carefully as the bear devours its victim's ear,
An unpleasant stench is very clear,
A smell I couldn't bear.

Kaila Mutenga (12)
St George's CE School, Gravesend

Change It Now

Why can't you see?
It's very clear,
glaciers are melting,
polar bears are even shedding tears.
We don't understand what our world could be,
we don't know what our Earth could see.
If we just looked after it, and recycled, please,
plastic, heat, we're burning up.
So, I'll ask you now, serious and free,
do you want to die or be able to see our future sea?
Animals going extinct,
it's only cruel.
Help them, instead of worrying about your jewels!
I'll say once again, this is not a drill,
change something now, or you'll be getting very ill.
Green, glorious trees falling to the ground,
no air left, suffocating all around.
I repeat, once again, this is not a drill,
let's all live and be kind to our town.

Emma Somerville (12)
Woodfarm High School, Thornliebank

Just Be You

Life.
Where do I start?
We were all built different sizes,
we never got to choose what we looked like
when we came down to Earth.
Even if you look different,
you still feel that little nudge to just fit in.
You do something daft to make someone laugh,
but you feel if you make that one mistake,
by saying this word: no!
Well you're wrong,
saying no can be good.
Just because this might mean you can't sit with the popular people,
because of that one word,
does not make you wrong,
because you are finally being yourself
and people will see that.
So be you.

Olivia Leask (12)
Woodfarm High School, Thornliebank

What Makes Me Perfect?

Every single breath I take,
The mirror makes my tummy ache.
Feeling worthless after every glare,
Why does everyone have to stare?
All I want is to be loved,
But that's not possible, is it?
Every single day and night,
Thinking that I don't look right,
What makes me perfect?

Blue eyes or green?
There's a difference between skinny and lean,
Why can't I love me?
Feeling trapped with this face,
Everyone makes fun of me,
Looking at all these girls,
Making me feel insecure.
But it always comes down to one thing,
What makes me perfect?

Olivia Bowie (12)
Woodfarm High School, Thornliebank

We Have A Voice

Listen to us speak
Listen to us shout
Our voices may be bleak
But we don't have a doubt
That our voices will be heard

Even if you say that we don't have a chance
We will rise up
We will take a stance
We will not give up
'Til the end, we will stand together

Even if you take our voices
Or even our chances
We will take them back
Even if you say we lack
What we need, we will fight together

We will have our say, our voice
We will change our world
We are the next generation
We have a voice.

Rachael Cassels (12)
Woodfarm High School, Thornliebank

One, Two, Three, Go!

If you think you are beaten, then you are,
If you think not to dare, then you don't win,
If you like to win but can't,
It's almost certain that you won't.

Push through, break the ice,
Trust me, you'll feel pretty nice,
Be the one who is fierce,
Be the one that is strong!

If you hear go but don't go,
It's going to be a big blow,
If you push through but fall,
Don't just roll into a big ball,
Just follow your dreams,
And go on one, two, three, go!

Rachel Somerville (12)
Woodfarm High School, Thornliebank

Perfect

Perfection is not real
and it's not set in steel.
We see all these people with perfect lips,
perfect shoes, perfect clothes,
and well, it's not real.
If you have ever seen a celeb online
and their food looks good
and clothes,
even make-up,
well, it's not real.
They probably have a designer with them.
So, when you are at home,
scrolling through your phone
at all these lovely,
non-realistic pictures,
don't change you, or anyone else.
Perfection is not real!

Lauren Glennie (12)
Woodfarm High School, Thornliebank

In The End It's Worth It

Be determined, no need to be afraid,
You are who you are,
And you can make what you make.
Don't give up on your dreams,
However tough they seem.
Keep on going,
Keep on knowing,
That you can do it,
Because, in the end, it's worth it!
Continue to persevere,
Then the end will be near,
Your goal can be in sight,
All you have to do is fight,
Fight for justice, not for fear,
Shout out loud for everyone to hear!
Because, in the end, it's worth it!

Ella Fontaniere (12)
Woodfarm High School, Thornliebank

The Plane

As the plane lands on the runway
And I just can't look away
Excitement rushing through my veins
Hoping it does not rain
On the plane
Finding my lane
Number 23
I might just wee
The kids are crying but I don't care because
I'm in the air!
Time feels slow when we land down low
In the vast Egyptian desert
Mummies under the ground
Tummy's rumbling, and I've found
A cute little kebab stall to satisfy my hunger.

Angus Robert Paxton (12)
Woodfarm High School, Thornliebank

Be Who You Are

Be who you are,
Follow your dreams,
No matter how hard life seems,
You will get far,
Be who you are,
No matter what you look like,
No matter what you act like,
Lock negative words in a jar,
Be who you are,
Don't let anyone bring you down,
Don't let anyone make you frown,
You will get far,
Be who you are,
Remember, you are strong,
Remember, it's okay to be wrong,
You are who you are.

Lily Monaghan (12)
Woodfarm High School, Thornliebank

Scrolling

Scrolling all day, scrolling, scrolling,
Endless models with their perfect bodies,
Perfect smiles, perfect hair, perfect face,
Perfect everything, and me... never perfect.

Scrolling all day, scrolling, scrolling,
Endless hate comments about my body,
My smile, my hair, my face, everything,
Unperfect.

Social media nightmare.

Crystal O'Hara (12)
Woodfarm High School, Thornliebank

Confidence

C onfidence is the key
O wn the world
N ever be who you are not
F ind the spark inside of you
I believe, so you should too
D on't be someone you're not
E veryone is taken
N ever let yourself down
C are about the nice comments
E njoy your life the way it is.

Hayah Ahmed (12)
Woodfarm High School, Thornliebank

If I Had A Magic Wand

If I had a magic wand,
I would do as I pleased,
I would ask for anything I wanted,
And it would appear,
I would ask for a dog,
There it would be,
I would ask for money,
And it would appear,
I would ask for a holiday,
I would be away,
If I had a magic wand,
Everything would be great.

Sophie Smith (12)
Woodfarm High School, Thornliebank

Bully

They do it daily,
and they will never stop.
Always teasing you about your interests.
Sometimes it can get physical,
and brutal.
It also happens at night,
your phone vibrating like mad,
because everyone knows they're going to stay bad.
You can change,
but you can't change a bully.

Murray Griffen (12)
Woodfarm High School, Thornliebank

What Makes Me, Me

I am who I am because
of my family,
they raised me and took care of me.
My friends,
they made me laugh
and showed me things I never knew.
My teachers,
they taught me and made me feel safe
where I am.
And that is what makes me,
me.

Conner Cai (12)
Woodfarm High School, Thornliebank

Climate Change

Ice warming,
Fire burning,
Heat, less for the bears to eat,
Burn, the world starts to turn,
Glacier, feel the wrath,
Flood, lots of blood,
Dying bees, more and more seas,
Earth to a crisp, just like a wisp.

Amy Motherwell (11)
Woodfarm High School, Thornliebank

The Break

Feeling weightless,
Light as a feather,
Soaring in the air,
Couldn't feel better.

Loud as a hurricane,
I heard a snap,
Seas of tears came down,
As my hand flew back.

Eva Miller (12)
Woodfarm High School, Thornliebank

My Idol
Haiku poetry

Danny Macaskill
Mountain biking, that is him
He is my idol

He does tricks so well
I watch all his videos
His tricks are so hard.

Euan Reid (12)
Woodfarm High School, Thornliebank

Friends

A haiku

Friends, we all need them
Kind, funny, make us laugh, cry,
Who could live without?

Alexander Ferns (12)
Woodfarm High School, Thornliebank